TECHNOLOGICAL
TERRORISM

In my ears are the cries of the stricken; and I can see, as I have seen in the past, all the marring and mangling of the sweet, beautiful flesh, and the souls torn with violence from proud bodies and hurled to God. Thus do we poor humans attain our ends, striving through carnage and destruction to bring lasting peace and happiness upon the earth.

— JACK LONDON in *The Iron Heel*

TECHNOLOGICAL TERRORISM

Richard Charles Clark

Foreword by Henry A. Paolucci

The Devin-Adair Company
Old Greenwich

For Phyllis, and

Agnes and Joseph

CONTENTS

Acknowledgments

My basic intellectual acknowledgment must be to St. Augustine of Hippo — in Bossuet's phrase "Eagle of Doctors" — especially in regard to order as the preeminent political value; and to those most responsible for transmitting to me and sustaining in me that Augustinian heritage: Professors Dino Bigoniari and Herbert A. Deane of Columbia University and especially Professor Henry A. Paolucci of St. John's University for a research leave in the fall of 1978 which enabled me to update the manuscript.

Foreword

ON OCTOBER 17, 1979, *The New York Times* carried an Associated Press report of interviews with eight security guards presently or formerly employed at the two nuclear power plants that make up the Consolidated Edison and State Power Authority facility at Indian Point, 24 miles north of New York City. The news-column headings read: "Guards Charge Security Is Lax At Indian Point. Inadequacies Held Threat — Allegations Denied." One guard had reportedly said: "It would take one commando or one well-trained wacko to go in, inflict heavy damage, and leave without being detected." Then he added: "To go in at nighttime, eliminate the guards and seize and hold the entire plant would take eight to 12 men. The way it's set up now, there's nothing to stop them."

The basic charge about deficiencies made by the guards served to highlight the extraordinary, but hardly unexpected, contrast at Indian Point between the advanced technology we all assume is being applied to produce nuclear power there and the essentially amateurish, virtually primitive procedures being pursued to hire, train, equip, and deploy the men and women who are supposed to guarantee the physical security — the effectively protected and serviceable possession — of such facilities for our general welfare as a sovereign people.

A main line of complaint of the interviewed guards was that, because of loose standards of selection for the security force at Indian Point — a looseness that permits the filing of falsified records of past employment, of training courses allegedly completed, of physical fitness, etc. — persons of manifest incompetence have lately been allowed "to fill key security slots." Speaking of the general run of new employees, one experienced guard said: "They're fine for department stores, but they don't belong at a nuclear plant. . . . Believe me, I'd never trust practically any one of them to back me up. They're either too fat, too old, or too dumb. . . . If we were ever attacked, it would be a joke."

There were reports of guards with drinking problems, of one in particular who liked to practice fast-drawing with a loaded gun, and of another who, apparently sober, "would take out his gun, unload it, aim at guards or other employees as they walked by and pull the trigger." Illustrating laxity of another, hardly less serious kind were reports of "female guards . . . granting free sexual favors to male workers, who sometimes lined up to wait their turn." According to a more detailed AP news account, "one such situation was ended only when a contractor asked that the women be moved to another post." Another time, a maintenance supervisor "looking for four of his guys" reportedly "found them in line with three other guys."

Responding to the published charges, spokesmen for the State Power Authority and Consolidated Edison noted that the guards at the Indian Point facilities are employees neither of the state nor of Con Ed, but of the Gleason Security Service in Hartsdale. At a press meeting representatives of the licensees, who bear ultimate responsibility for plant security, protested that "security at Indian Point meets NRC [Nuclear Regulatory Commission] requirements." Power Authority officials,

the AP report of mid-October concluded, "refused to discuss specifics but generally denied the allegations made
by the guards. They said they would investigate any alleged improprieties, especially those concerning falsified
records." Meanwhile, they would acknowledge only that
the "security staff — composed mostly of young men and
retirees — is inexperienced because of a high turnover
rate of 20 percent [those with one year's seniority are
considered 'old-timers'], which a commission official attributed to low pay, long hours and the tedium of the job."
What resulted from official investigation of the charges
was briefly reported in the *Times* a month later: The
entire security force at Indian Point had been dismissed,
and that was the end of the news story — though not of the
problem.

The problem as such, the problem of technological security in this technocratic age of ours — viewed in full
perspective and not simply in the aspects of personnel
efficiency suggested in the news item we have just examined — is the theme of this extraordinarily thorough
study by Richard Charles Clark. A polymath in research
and prolific scholarly writer in many fields, including
literary criticism, he has previously published a series of
major articles on aspects of this subject, titles of which
include: "The Response to Terrorism," "Terrorism and the
Media," "Crisis Government," "The Urban-Guerrilla
Threat," "It Can't Happen Here," "A Question of Means,"
"Hypocrisy on Gun-Control," and "The Crisis of Liberal
Democracy." More recently, adaptations of portions of the
present volume were published in *State of the Nation* as
separate articles titled "Prometheus Unbound," "The
Apollo Diversions," and "An Accumulation of Troubles,"
while a paper summarizing its major implications, but
emphasizing "Constitutional Crisis Remedies," was read
at the Northeastern Political Science Association Annual

Meeting of November 8-10, 1979, held at Newark, New Jersey.

As more and more groups around the world (whether in the employ of First or Second or Third World governments or on their own) acquire skill in the arts of terrorist political blackmail, the theme becomes increasingly timely. Events of our time amply confirm James Reston's prediction (cited at length later in this volume) that before long our chief national-security worries may have less to do with "cruise missiles, backfire bombers, and neutron artillery shells that can kill fleets of tanks" than with the kinds of technological terror which "desperate minorities" or well-trained commando units operating covertly in our midst are now increasingly capable of unleashing. And the responses to Professor Clark's sharp recommendations have as a consequence become increasingly positive.

In its broadest historical perspective, his central thesis can be simply put as follows: Republics or commonwealths are usually built up or accumulated (as the etymologies imply) by collective industry and trade, or, more properly, by productive activity subordinated to a common will. They have traditionally come into being, as Aristotle long ago observed, to guarantee *mere* life, on a communally shared basis. But they make themselves worthy of continued existence — supported by an affectionately consensual common will — only in the measure that they make possible a well-directed or *good* life. Yet that isn't the whole story. What needs to be emphatically stressed for our time is the hard fact that a technologically well-produced commonwealth, like that of our two-hundred-year-old national union, needs to be well protected — routinely and habitually — before it can be well directed.

Do we have a routinely and habitually well-protected commonwealth? Here it must be said that, judged by performance (as documented in the chapters of this book), the answer has to be no. The corporate managers and high Government officers directly charged with providing for the defense of our technologically advanced national productivity appear, by and large, to have been as inefficiently recruited, trained, equipped, and deployed as the general run of security guards who have recently lost their jobs at the Indian Point, N.Y., nuclear facilities.

Back in 1972 Professor Clark noted how closely allied were the visions of an ideal world to come entertained by the heads of our industrial corporate giants — the Dow Chemical Company, for instance — and their chief "campus critics" of the time. Speaking apologetically at a White House conference, Dow Chairman Carl A. Gerstacker had in fact protested that his company then had a bad reputation among academicians largely because, "through no fault of its own," it had to some extent to serve at home and abroad as "an instrument of American policy." His company's corporate ideal, he said approvingly, ran in a different direction. Dow's high aim was rather to staff its top offices with "multinational bees," streaming into it out of all countries, whose skills and temperaments (developed through long years of international employment) would eventually enable the company as a whole to escape the coils of traditional national loyalties.

Asserting that American Big Business was "moving strongly" in the direction of not just multinational companies, as we know them today, but toward "anational companies — companies without nationality, belonging to all nationalities," Chairman Gerstacker then asked his audience to join him in a cosmopolitan reverie, which, as an expression of rootless antinational detachment, was certainly a worthy "capitalist" counterpart of Karl Marx's stirring appeal to the proletarians of the world to unite themselves, as rootless exploited workers, against the governments of all nations. In sonorously cadenced speech he thus presented Dow's version of Hollywood's more traditional island paradises: "Visualize an island somewhere in international waters, alive with activity, launches rushing back and forth ferrying executives and white collar workers to a sprawling office complex housing the world headquarters of the Dow Chemical Company. Because it is outside national boundaries, the company is subject to the laws of no single nation or society, but is free to operate all over the world under the rules governing the domestic competition in each country it enters."

One should perhaps recall at this point that, when the old East India Company first established its world headquarters in the Bengal region of India in times long past, its extranational status was pretty much of the kind here projected for his own Honorable Company by Mr. Gerstacker. "The British came to trade," as Sir Percival Spear so pointedly sums up the long tale in his *Oxford History of Modern India: 1740-1947,* "and went into politics to preserve their trade." What sort of politics might we expect a Mr. Gerstacker to pursue, once it became clear that his denationalized company business needed to provide more deliberately, as the old East India Company did, for its common defense? What sort of guards could a Mr. Gerstacker expect to recruit to secure the safety of his very special island?

The obvious answer is that, before long, the island would have ceased to be Dow's; all high-technology production or communications systems would have ceased to function, the painstakingly gathered "multinational bees" would have been driven off, replaced first by clench-fisted, chanting religious zealots, perhaps, and then by ideologically disciplined producers of cruder commonwealths whose recruiters would certainly not have neglected the arts of effectively protecting what they have arranged to produce.

That is the sort of lesson to be learned from this powerful book. In his *Physics and Politics,* written for the benefit of Englishmen shortly after our tragic Civil War, Walter Bagehot thus summed up a comparable lesson: "History is strewn with the wrecks of nations which have gained a little progressiveness at the cost of a great deal of hard manliness, and have thus prepared themselves for destruction as soon as the movements of the world gave a chance for it."

— HENRY A. PAOLUCCI

New York, January, 1980

GLOSSARY

AEC	Atomic Energy Commission
DOE	Department Of Energy
DOT	Department Of Transportation
ERDA	Energy Research and Development Agency
GAO	General Accounting Office
FAA	Federal Aviation Administration
FCC	Federal Communications Commission
FPC	Federal Power Commission
IAEA	International Atomic Energy Agency
ICC	Interstate Commerce Commission
LEAA	Law Enforcement Assistance Administration
LEG	Liquefied Energy Gas
LNG	Liquefied Natural Gas
LPG	Liquefied Propane Gas
MUF	Missing and Unaccounted For
NIHS	National Institutes of Health Sciences
NRC	Nuclear Regulatory Commission
NSA	National Security Agency
SSA	Social Security Administration

Introduction

TERRORISM as a weapon of crime or political ambition has had a long and varied past. The concern of this small volume is, however, with its future. For it is possible, indeed probable, that the political variety of terrorism will before long become a problem transcending all others, subsuming all others, and making all others, by comparison, pale in significance.

We must say this because of the advent of technological terrorism. Having crossed the threshhold of what Zbigniew Brzezinski has called the Technocratic Age, terrorism has now taken up weapons of mass destruction whose effectiveness can be measured only in terms of megadeaths. Such instruments of destruction have been given us, as we all know, by a "benevolent" science. It is Mary Shelley's Frankenstein allegory realizing itself in history.

This book's purpose is threefold: to indicate convincingly the potential magnitude of the problem; to document and thereby substantiate our charge of an almost blanket lack of response to the problem by all branches of the Federal Government involved, both elective and bureaucratic; and to anticipate the possible political and social implications of the actuality of large-scale technological terrorism — or even its mere possibility or threat — in a traditionally free society of government by discussion, like our own.

In the 1960's we were treated to an abundance of writings, many quite romanticized, on guerrilla warfare. The universities and professors "retooled" and worked the etiologies of discontent and the "Che Guevaras" into their courses. By the 1970's, when the most significant guerrilla wars (those in Indochina and, following the Portuguese withdrawal, in Africa) had been lost, largely by default through lack of the moral will to continue the struggle, experts at all levels and the media became preoccupied with urban terrorism.

Their preoccupation is, as we intend to demonstrate, misdirected. New instruments of mass destruction are now readily at hand. Yet to the extent that mass technological terrorism has received any attention at all, the focus is largely on nuclear terrorism, and then, oftener than not, in the form of media entertainments for mass market consumption. In fact, chemical, bacteriological, and biological instruments are much easier to fabricate than nuclear weapons, and thus more likely to be used. They are referred to in "the trade" as the poor man's atom bombs.

In considering technological terrorism there are three basic questions the reader should bear in mind:

1. Is the technical knowledge available, and to whom and at what level of expertise?
2. Are the materials available?
3. Is the willingness to use these instruments present?

Technological terrorism is horrifying to contemplate. The threat, as Lowell Ponte, a recognized specialist in research on bizarre weapons, has stressed, is real and awesome. Brian Jenkins, an expert on terrorism for the Rand Corporation, has warned that in the very near future terrorists will be hijacking not aircraft but entire cities or even nations. The water supply systems, food supplies, transportation, communications, and energy for large metropolitan areas are highly vulnerable and virtually unguarded.

Naive faith in the uninterrupted functioning of this technology is widespread. At his press conference immediately prior to a much-publicized journey on a nuclear submarine President Carter was asked whether it might not be imprudent for him to be aboard any vessel for such a long period. He replied by assuring the nation that while aboard the sub he would be in constant communication with the command and control centers in Washington. There was no reason for concern, he stressed. However, it has been well known for many years within the intelligence communities that the entire nuclear submarine system (which is a principal component of our nuclear deterrent) can be interdicted rather easily by sabotaging as few as four installations or by electronically jamming the radio communications systems. Ironically, only a few days earlier *The New York Times* had reported (May 15, 1977) in a brief story that "after almost twenty years of searching, the Navy still has no place to put Project Seafarer, a proposed low-frequency radio system to communicate with submerged submarines." It seems that such systems cause environmental damage and physical problems for animals and humans. There has thus been strong opposition from each locale where the Navy has attempted to place the system. As the *Times* noted: "The Navy wants the system because it is theoretically unjammable and could be received deep under water worldwide." Carter's confidence in uninterrupted communication was, it seems, misplaced. Somebody once formulated a law that explains Carter's (and most other people's) naive trust in the proper functioning of technology: To the nonexpert any highly advanced technology is indistinguishable from magic. We assume that the experts have constructed technologically fail-safe systems to handle all problems.

If this can happen to such a high-priority system, imagine the ease with which civilian installations may be rendered inoperative and the resultant chaos that would ensue. Imagine, for example, the upheaval if both the Saudi pipeline and the Alaska pipeline were seriously sabotaged.

What has the Government's response to this threat been? In the area of nuclear terrorism, which has received the most discussion — although even that has been inadequate — all Federal agencies concerned have been grossly derelict in their responsibilities, and, worse, some have at times engaged in a massive cover-up. Unlike the Watergate cover-up, this one can materially affect the lives of all Americans and others in the non-Communist industrial nations.

The involved branches of the Federal Government, in particular the NRC and the ERDA, have insisted time after time over the past five years that they are going to do the day after tomorrow what they had previously assured us time after time they had done the day before yesterday. The sole exception to this political-bureaucratic fiasco is the GAO (General Accounting Office), which has consistently warned in lengthy documented reports of the general lack of security at both Government and civilian atomic plants, and brought to public attention the fact that large amounts of weapons-grade nuclear materials are missing. Even the GAO, however, has made its share of inconsistent statements.

A terrorist group's capacity to engage in nuclear terrorism is dependent upon technological expertise and obtaining weapons-grade materials. For years Government spokesmen denied that the technical knowledge was readily available or that it could be mastered by potential terrorists. More recently, they have conceded that the technology *is* available and that the fabrication of a bomb is not especially difficult, but that the materials are not available because of "increasingly stringent security precautions." If the latter denial is untrue — which it is — then our security depends solely upon the humanitarian impulses of the terrorist, the psychotic, and the criminal.

Most of all, the media has been seriously derelict in its attention to the subject. Its spokesmen have largely ignored a massive threat of almost indescribable proportions, a threat that can easily wrench us out of our current political-social-economic structures and effect a change in our lives greater than that from feudalism to capitalism, but in an incredibly more accelerated time span.

In general, the more prominent and influential analysts of terrorism do not take this view. Typical are the concluding remarks of J. Bowyer Bell in his AEI-Hoover Institution policy study, *Transnational Terror* (1975):

> Terrorist incidents may produce horror and indignation, but actual systemic disruption is minimal. Airlines still fly, passengers still wait in transit lounges, and the cargo gets through. Major cities withstood much more devastating assaults in World War II than could ever be managed by terrorists. . . . The real effect of terrorist action on the transnational system will always be more a matter of appearance than of reality. The toll of the terrorist is more comparable to the rate of auto fatalities than to the slaughter of conventional war. Even in Northern Ireland, more people die on the highways than by terror.
>
> The system, far from being rigid, is in truth amply pliable and can absorb the various terrorist threats. There is a variety of defenses as well as a mix of responses possible, but because of the dread nature of these new revolutionary acts, the general reaction has been deeply emotional rather than practical. This vast indignation provides a poor foundation for what is clearly going to be a continuing and perhaps escalating assault on world order.

We do not accept this typical view. Throughout history weaponry has undergone certain technological developments that have always been intimately related to whoever holds political power in a state. And that is because the ultimate source of political authority is coercive power. In the Homeric period of classical Greece the virtuoso knights were the dominant force. But to be a knight required a certain economic substance. One needed sufficient wealth for a horse and the long period of training required to learn how to use the weapons. During the Middle Ages that was also true. But then came the great democratic invention of firearms. Firearms required little skill to use, and made each person equal to everyone else. To this day, among criminal subcultures and the military, the firearm is still referred to as "an equalizer." But then came yet more sophisticated firearms, which in turn led to aristocratic-oligarchic political effects. Automatic weapons, artillery, and air power were usually beyond the scope of the average person. And then in 1945 came atomic weaponry. That seemed to mean that now the most powerful nations would dominate the world, and permanently. Since then another great "democratic" advance has been made in weapons technology. Nuclear weapons, as well as biological and chemical ones, are now readily available to those who have the will to use them.

It is the purpose of this work to establish that these instruments of mass destruction *are* easily available. More important, it is our intention to demonstrate that the Government, the media, and the intelligentsia have not, for the most part, made any significant response to a problem that concerns life itself for us all.

PART I

Nuclear Terrorism

1. Early Warnings and Denials

ONLY recently has the doleful horror of nuclear terrorism
received any attention at all from the media. The Government, in what amounts to a vast bureaucratic cover-up
in self-defense, continues to insist that all necessary precautions have been taken. But the chronology of events
over the past several years reveals clearly that only a few
totally ineffectual precautions have in fact been taken.
This chronology amounts to a severe indictment of the
bureaucracy, the Congress, the Pentagon, the Department of Defense, the media, and the United Nations. It is
an especially severe indictment of the NRC (Nuclear Regulatory Commission), previously the AEC (Atomic
Energy Commission), which emerges as a "ship of fools." It
is a singularly astounding story.

Concern about nuclear terrorism was made public in 1973 after former high-ranking officials and scientists had their warnings contemptuously dismissed by the Pentagon and other agencies. Until then "diversion" (theft) of "special nuclear materials" (weapons-grade materials) was largely a matter for James Bond-type entertainments in which a military nuclear weapon would be stolen. But those weapons were at least under heavy military guard. During the 1970's, however, the number of civilian nuclear power plants was expected to grow from 37 in 1973 to 185 by 1985, with at least an equal number abroad. That would cause a rapid buildup of the amount of plutonium, a waste product that can be recycled or used in other rather interesting ways, such as the construction of a nuclear bomb. There thus emerged the great risk of theft, since neither the civilian nor Government nuclear power plants had anywhere near the security of military weapons on bases.

In a then unpublished Ford Foundation report, prepared largely by Dr. Theodore B. Taylor, a nuclear weapons expert, and submitted in hearings before the Joint Committee on Atomic Energy in September, 1973, it was emphasized that only a few pounds of special nuclear materials were necessary to make a rather powerful bomb. Significantly, and perhaps imprudently, those hearings were made available to the public, and to anyone who desired to use the information.

AEC officials were pressed for their comments on the reports. Manning Huntzing, the AEC's Director of Regulation, uttered the first of what was to become a long litany of misleading and even false claims by asserting that the report "does not reflect" stiffened regulations announced by the AEC earlier in 1973 for transporting plutonium from the civilian plants in heavily guarded, armed, alarm-equipped trucks in much the same way that military weapons material has been moved. He neglected to point out that regulations "announced" by the AEC are not necessarily put into effect.

Rules issued in 1970, Huntzing assured the public, required that more than eleven pounds of highly concentrated U-235 and unspecified quantities of plutonium must be stored in a locked building equipped with at least alarms that could summon guards quickly. (That is about the same level of security people provide for their garden tools.) Earlier in 1973, he stressed, the AEC had issued "proposed" new rules for transportation going beyond earlier requirements that no shipments should be made in passenger airliners that could be hijacked and that the AEC be immediately notified if a shipment failed to arrive on schedule. We must then conclude that prior to this it was *not* necessary to notify the AEC if a shipment of weapons-grade materials did not arrive. Under the *proposed* new rules armed guards would now accompany rail and truck shipments, unless the truck was of a special design, having special features resistant to penetration and enabling immobilization of the vehicle in the case of attempted theft. Huntzing was, of course, talking about a Brink's-type armored truck, which can be hijacked rather easily merely by being put into a tractor-trailer truck, as we have seen on TV shows.

Similarly, AEC Commissioner Kriegsman attempted to tranquilize the nation by downgrading the gravity of the problem in his testimony:

> The national security and public safety problems created by a rapid expansion of nuclear power plants . . . are real, yet, when placed in perspective, they are manageable. . . . The major threat involves only a few steps of the entire fuel cycle for short periods of time.

But, as Taylor had pointed out months earlier (March 14, 1973) in a speech to the Scientific Research Society of

America, those new regulations appeared to offer less impediment to theft than had been successfully overcome by several criminal groups in the past, such as those responsible for the Brink's, the Great Train, the Ontario Rockville Trust, and, more recently, the New York City Police Department (heroin) robberies.

Early in 1974 a Ford Foundation report by Mason Willrich and Theodore B. Taylor was published under the title *Nuclear Theft: Risks and Safeguards*. To achieve maximum distribution it was put out in paperback at a minimal price. As Taylor later acknowledged, in order to prove how easy it was to make a nuclear bomb, it was necessary for him to include relevant information for the actual construction of one. In short, his warning was also a primer. Concening the possibility of nuclear blackmail, the report stressed that present safeguards are inadequate and urged the establishment of a special security force to prevent theft of nuclear materials. It emphasized that only a small number of attackers could steal fissionable material, such as plutonium, from trucks, laboratories, and processing plants. With that material "an explosive atomic device would be relatively easy to make," and might even be made by one inventive person working alone. Even the crudest, low-yield weapon would kill tens of thousands and cause millions of dollars in property damage. Willrich, as a lawyer, was involved in the legal aspects of weapons. Taylor, a physicist, had helped design weapons used at Los Alamos from 1949 to 1956, and had then become a critic of nuclear power programs, although he was not in favor of suspending them. He was trying to prod the Government into taking more stringent preventive measures. The increasing concern at this time was related to the activities of the Palestinian guerrillas in the Middle East.

In response to that book the AEC said that meanwhile it had strengthened safeguard requirements. Nevertheless, as more nuclear materials were being produced, "existing safeguard requirements may, in the future, need to be upgraded." Speaking "informally" to a *New York Times* reporter, an AEC spokesman said that "we're not arguing with them. It's a matter of timing — how much you do and when." Willrich had pointed out that the civilian nuclear industry had given serious consideration to the idea of a Federal security service, which, he said, was more than had been forthcoming from the AEC in regard to Federal power plants.

The essence of the debate, according to the *Times*, was whether "unauthorized persons" could fashion a nuclear device, and how much special knowledge and equipment they would need. Taylor — and it bears reemphasizing that he is an expert on nuclear weapons — said that he had challenged the AEC to assign a small group of volunteers with some scientific background to the task of designing a homemade bomb, given the assumption that fissionable materials could be stolen. The design, he said, could then be subjected to computer tests, or the AEC could even build and try out the device. In *Nuclear Theft* Taylor and Willrich maintained that the necessary materials (other than fissionable matter and some high explosives) can be bought from hardware stores and commercial suppliers of scientific equipment for high schools. They therefore strongly urged that a safeguard system be designed that could deflect a "maximum credible threat." At this time "maximum credible threat" was being defined as "an attack of a group of perhaps five to ten persons using sophisticated firearms and equipment."

Scarcely three weeks after the AEC had vigorously denied all charges and soothingly reassured everyone that stringent safeguards were now in effect it completely reversed itself. On April 26, 1974, the AEC issued a report warning of the peril of terrorists stealing weapons-grade nuclear materials. It now belatedly admitted that safeguards were "entirely inadequate." And the danger, it gloomily warned, was large and growing because of the increasing dissemination "of precise and accurate instructions on how to make simple nuclear weapons and increasing professional skills, intelligence networks, finances, and level of armaments of terrorist groups throughout the world." The report, written by three scientists and two law enforcement specialists, had been intended for internal consumption only, but it was released by the Joint Committee for Atomic Energy. In short, the AEC had been saying one thing publicly and something quite different privately. In recent years, it emphatically stressed, the factors that make safeguards a real, imminent, and vital issue had changed rapidly for the worse. It cited the growth of Arab terrorism, urban terrorist groups in Latin America, and the SLA in the U.S.

The AEC therefore recommended certain steps to increase the safeguards. A conspicuous feature of these "increased safeguards" is their inadequacy. The main ones follow:

1. Designing a system to protect our "estimate of the maximum credible threat," which was now being defined as an attack by fifteen highly trained men on a facility storing or transporting nuclear material. (One can only speculate as to the basis used to arrive at the number fifteen.)
2. Setting up a Federal nuclear protection and transportation service and upgrading the present protection system by forming a "small Federal force" trained to respond to theft.
3. Setting up an intelligence network with "continual and strong liaison" with the CIA and FBI.
4. Development of "threat scenarios" to test the adequacy of protection through "gaming" analysis. (That, of course, would provide employment for a number of out-of-work

Ph. D.'s. But since it would be impossible to maintain the security of such threat scenarios in the age of "government-by-leak," they could obviously be used by the terrorist groups themselves.)
5. Tightening accounting procedures to locate losses immediately.
6. Developing "double contingency" when measuring plutonium and uranium in and out of the processing steps with two independent observers to check each other.
7. Development of a system of daily, precise measurements and counting of nuclear materials.
(The last three measures reveal the total inadequacy, at that time, of safeguards.)

The report concluded by emphasizing that "the potential harm to the public from the explosion of an illicitly made nuclear weapon is greater than from any plausible power plant accident, including one which involves a core meltdown and subsequent breach of containment." Unfortunately, it was the lesser threat, of a power plant accident involving a core meltdown, that was receiving most of the publicity in the media and in bestselling horror books on how we almost lost Detroit. The public issuance of such a report, as of all other reports on this subject, has a double effect: While alerting the people to the dangers of nuclear terrorism it also alerts the terrorists to their exciting options.

Senator Ribicoff, properly so in our opinion, justified the release of the AEC report on the ground that "the general public is entitled to know of the serious danger posed by the failure of the AEC to institute an adequate safeguard system." He withheld, whether naively or as a posture, the section describing possible scenarios for breaching the system of protecting nuclear materials, noting that it was classified. (Though, as we all know, newspapers commonly and casually publish secret documents on their front pages, to say nothing of those that are merely "classified." Some columnists, such as Jack Anderson, seem to publish little but secret documents.) Ribicoff then sponsored a bill to upgrade protection of plutonium and uranium, and to reorganize the agency.

Five days later (May 1, 1974) the AEC ordered utilities to arm their guards. So casual was the AEC about security that until this time the men "guarding" weapons-grade nuclear materials were not even armed.

The reaction of the civilian nuclear industry to that "order" was interesting. Many utilities, including Con Edison of New York, protested that the weapons would add new dangers from accidents. The AEC had based its order on a study that had cited "recent trends of violence by certain subcultures of modern society." According to *The New York Times*, despite their protest the utilities said they were going to go along with the order. What is rather surprising as well as dismaying is that the utilities evidently could have said that they were *not* going to go along with the order.

With some justification the utilities had objected to providing their own armed guards, contending that protecting nuclear plants from sabotage was a national defense function. "The industry," Dr. James A. Powers, Chief of the AEC's Materials Protection Standards Branch, reported, "does not feel that it should be responsible for the common defense of the country." But the AEC had decided, he said, that if nuclear power is to be developed privately, private industry will have to shoulder the security burden at the plants. One high industry source, who refused to be quoted by name, according to the *Times*, said that the companies were concerned over such potentially dangerous situations as "sabotage, terrorist actions, and blackmail threats." They were concerned, too, over the arming of the guards, "because the caliber of industrial guards is not very high — they're not exactly an elite corps." Furthermore, he indignantly complained, "in the presence of delicate machinery, you don't like to provoke a gun battle." That high industry source obviously felt that it is better to let terrorists steal weapons-grade materials for a homemade bomb than to sustain possible damage to their expensive, delicate machinery. Security for nuclear materials, it seems, would have to await resolution of the dispute over who was willing to pay for it.

The AEC's requirements were based on a ten-page set of standards, "Industrial Security for Nuclear Power Plants," issued in 1973. But, as we noted earlier, those rules were only "proposed" by the AEC in 1973. They had been developed by the American National Standards Institute, Inc., a private concern. The standards are, the Institute says, very general because "specific provisions of industrial security programs must be regarded as highly sensitive information." On the question of guns, the manual says:

> The extent to which the [security] forces are supplied with protective equipment such as firearms, tear gas, crowd control devices, or nightsticks [sic], as well as the duties assigned these forces, must be carefully assessed by the owner organization. The merits of arming security forces to meet threats . . . shall be carefully weighed against the potential hazards associated with possible misuse of firearms.

What that means is that the directors of the individual plants have the prerogative to decide whether even to arm their guards as they weigh the risk of damage to their costly equipment.

It has long been a truism in the field of political science that the so-called independent regulatory commissions function basically as creatures of the industry they are supposed to control or regulate, whether it be the FAA, the FCC, or the AEC. According to this manual, developed not by a government security agency but by a private firm, a nuclear plant security system should be able "to respond to a wide variety of potential threats," ranging from a "single disgruntled employee" to "spontaneous and undisciplined actions of a relatively large group of people involved in mob activities associated with civil disturbance." Most important, they caution that some protection is beyond the scope of a private company: "Protection against actions associated with deliberate assaults by trained para-military groups or military units of a foreign power is not covered by this standard. Protection against such actions is the responsibility of the U.S. Government."

By this time one would have thought that the AEC would have been aware of the imperative danger of the threat. However, the AEC gave nuclear plant operators till March 6 to come up with a plan for individual plants, with the new procedures generally to go into effect by June 15 — almost a year later. If the AEC *was* taking the problem seriously, then its response was criminally negligent at best; if it was not, then its behavior was even worse.

In mid-1974 John McPhee published *The Curve of Binding Energy*, the text of which had originally appeared in *The New Yorker*. On July 9 it was reviewed by Christopher Lehmann-Haupt in *The New York Times* under the title "An Atom Bomb in Every Home." The problem with mass media book reviewers is that they assume a posture of competency in any field, no matter how ignorant of that field they may be. The thrust of Lehmann-Haupt's review, as was the case with most organs of the mass media, was to pooh-pooh the whole matter:

Instead of exploring in delightful depth some relatively shallow subject — as he has done so often in his previous books — Mr. McPhee has brought us a frightening message of potential doom. This time he has explored the world of a theoretical physicist named Theodore B. Taylor. It is Dr. Taylor's main professional concern at the moment to convey to the American public his belief that with the growing availability of fissionable nuclear material and declassified technical know-how, it is now not only feasible for almost any country in the world to fabricate an atomic bomb, but it is also possible for smaller groups of individuals to do so as well. Indeed, in Dr. Taylor's highly competent judgment, it is not inconceivable that a single person could put together an atomic weapon in the privacy of his home laboratory. . . . Dr. Taylor is, to say the least, an interesting figure. In 1949, he went straight from failing his doctoral exams at the California Institute of Technology to designing more efficient fission bombs at Los Alamos; among them were Davy Crockett, "which in its time was the lightest and smallest fission bomb ever made," and the Super Oralloy Bomb, according to Mr. McPhee "the largest-yield fission bomb that has ever been exploded anywhere." Later he undertook the design of an interplanetary rocket ship that was to be as large as a sixteen-story building and propelled by shock waves from a series of atomic explosions — a project that had the support of no less than Niels Bohr, Harold Urey, Curtis LeMay, Hans Bethe and Wernher von Braun, among others (and a project that was only suspended with the implementation of the limited-test-ban treaty of 1963). . . . One cannot help thinking it no wonder that in Dr. Taylor's maturity he is obsessed with people building and setting off illicit bombs. And this, despite the cogency of his reasoning and the clarity with which Mr. McPhee has illustrated it, is at least one major point on the side of those who disagree with Dr. Taylor and argue that his obsession is "more a James Bond fear than a real one" or that, as James R. Schlesinger put it when he was chairman of the Atomic Energy Commission, "a self-respecting terrorist has better things to do than to take nuclear material" and construct homemade atomic bombs.

Thus did the *Times* reviewer alert its readers to the dangers, describing Taylor's warnings as "extreme" and as an "obsession." Considering Schlesinger's current reputation as the great realist, that quote from him is also all the more significant. Significant too is the fact that less than a year later John McPhee was to argue that Taylor was not an alarmist, that, if anything, he was understating the case.

In September, 1974, yet another danger in regard to nuclear terrorism became public. It was revealed that in the crisis over Cyprus the United States had issued standby orders to Marines to rescue its nuclear warheads, having "extreme concern" over their security. Stockpiles of nuclear warheads in both Greece and Turkey were customarily protected, it was now revealed, by only very small detachments of U.S. troops. It was clear that in a war, a civil war, or a revolution, those stockpiles could easily be taken by elements of any armed force.

In the wake of Congressional criticism of their vulnerability to terrorist attack, the Pentagon announced (September 26, 1974) plans to add to nuclear arms security. It was revealed that 7,000 tactical nuclear weapons were stored in Europe, *many under the protective custody of local governments*. A bewildered Representative Clarence Long (D. Md.) of the Appropriations Committee reported that the Pentagon had said that it needed 90 million dollars or more to provide such security, yet had requested only 4.9 million dollars for that purpose. General Davison, Commander of U.S. Army Europe, publicly complained that security measures were being hampered by the lack of funds. Even with increased substantive security changes following the terrorist attack at the Munich Olympic Village, "it would be difficult to protect any target which was the objective of a well-trained and properly armed and maniacal group. Other security measures should be taken, but the funds are unavailable." Representative Long, as a result of his own investigation conducted over six months, concluded that there "were serious security deficiencies at many U.S. nuclear weapons sites in the domestic United States, Europe, and Asia." The Joint Committee on Atomic Energy had reached a similiar conclusion, and for two years had been pressing the Pentagon to improve security. Long said he found it "puzzling" that the Pentagon had failed to ask for more than 4.9 million dollars, "because the sums involved are not huge compared to some wasted on officers clubs, commissaries, air-conditioning, and other noncombat-oriented items."

In response, William Beecher, Department of Defense spokesman, said that the Pentagon was planning "substantial additional" measures over the next few years, probably exceeding 90 million dollars. But, good bureaucrat that he was, he said that even without the additional measures the nuclear weapons were relatively secure. James R. Schlesinger, by this time moved up to Secretary of Defense, continuing to downplay the threat, said at a news conference that there was "low risk of any penetration" by terrorist groups. The Joint Committee on Atomic Energy vehemently disputed the confidence of the Pentagon. In a statement on the floor of the Senate, Senator Pastore, Vice-Chairman, said that despite "certain improvements, certain sites continue to appear to be vulnerable to terrorist attack." Representative Long concurred, noting that in one country, which he left unidentified, nuclear weapons were stored less than 250 feet from "a slum which has harbored dissidents for years."

We now shift back to the problem of security in the civilian nuclear industry. One week after those Congressional warnings the headlines of a major story in the *Times* read: "Congress and Administration Agree on Atom Security." The Joint Committee on Atomic Energy (which, it will be recalled, under the leadership of Senator Ribicoff had been in the forefront of warnings about the danger of nuclear theft) and the Ford Administration agreed to a *major slash* in an *urgently* requested security program designed to lessen the chances of theft of nuclear materials. The *Times* reported that the new program (now rejected) had been proposed by the AEC in May, 1974, after two studies by the GAO asserted that existing security measures were inadequate and several scientists had published reports concluding that a band of terrorists could transform a small amount of plutonium or uranium into a bomb. The AEC had requested 87 million dollars. That would have enabled it to hire three hundred additional guards. (That would come out to approximately seven-and-a-half additional guards for each of the forty plants then in existence, or about two per eight-hour shift.) It would also have enabled them to install new alarm and detector systems, construct improved fences and tamper-proof shipping cases, and to purchase additional equipment to track nuclear materials if stolen. Rejecting that proposal by the AEC, President Ford's White House Office of Management and Budget sent Congress a recommendation for 18 million dollars, 69 million dollars less than that urged by the AEC, which in itself was not exactly extravagant in the light of the consequences of theft of weapons-grade nuclear materials. Senator Ribicoff's "security-minded" Joint Committee agreed to restore 5 million dollars, if sustained by Congress. The total would be one-third the amount recommended by the AEC.

General Gillen, the AEC's Assistant General Manager for National Security, explained to the press the effects of the budget cut. The AEC could purchase no extra detection material to search for stolen materials. At that time it had one complete set, in the Midwest, and it had requested two additional sets. It could not hire the three hundred additional guards. It could not finance any research program for satellite-assisted communications systems. It could not establish any computerized inventory systems to enable it to know the exact location of all materials at all times. (Computerized inventory systems are also subject to penetration-manipulation, as we shall see.)

By way of background the *Times* summarized those earlier GAO reports. The first, issued in November, 1973, stated that the GAO had uncovered plants with inadequate security. By "inadequate security" they meant "weak fences, ineffective patrols, lack of automatic detection devices, and no plan should material be stolen." The second, issued in April, 1974, described how they had followed the shipment of three large loads of enriched uranium, and concluded that "the material was subject to diversion." Both reports said that only 34 pounds of uranium or 16 pounds of plutonium were required to fashion a crude nuclear device, but that 2.2 million pounds were expected to be in circulation by 1980. That poundage is much disputed. Many nuclear physicists contend that much less is needed to make a nuclear bomb. The GAO reports also thoroughly rejected, at this time, the opinion of Taylor. The reports insisted that a bomb could not be made by an amateur machinist or TV-type electronics technician. The reports did, however, cite *one* nuclear physicist who said it could be done by a sufficiently dedicated band of bomb-makers.

Two-and-a-half months later (December 28, 1974) *The New York Times* reported in a major story that

> thousands of pounds of nuclear materials were *unaccounted for*. Neither the AEC nor the civilian nuclear power industry could account for them. Although the officials insisted that there are now no unresolved cases of theft, the AEC was unable to give positive assurances that the missing materials had not fallen into the hands of a terrorist group or hostile government. They maintained that it was missing only in the sense that it was embedded in processing machinery or lost in the crude statistical methods used to keep track of the material. But they cautioned that with only forty pounds [it is now up to "only forty pounds"] of enriched uranium or twelve pounds of plutonium, a small group of people could make a

bomb capable of killing thousands. [As our chronicle develops, the poundage keeps going up and the deaths keep going down.] But most important, the AEC cautioned that "because of widespread dissemination of instructions for processing special nuclear materials [weapons grade] and for making simple nuclear weapons [courtesy of freedom of the press], *acquisition of special nuclear materials remains the only substantial problem* facing groups desiring to have such weapons" (emphasis added).

By now the AEC was rejecting its own earlier position, as well as the position of the GAO, that private groups or persons cannot make a bomb. It was admitting what it had previously denied, that bombs can be made easily. But it was still insisting that it had more than adequate security. The *Times,* in a misleading report, described certain developments that had occurred "despite the increasingly stringent regulations" in force. It neglected to add that those "increasingly stringent regulations" involved such things as giving pistols to "rent-a-cops." Thus:

Despite the increasingly stringent regulations concerning the control of enriched uranium and plutonium, a federal official who asked not to be indentified told *The New York Times* that there were two known instances where government employees were discovered to have smuggled out of guarded facilities enough special nuclear materials to fashion a nuclear weapon. The official refused to make public any further details about the cases. According to one knowledgeable official, an employee working in a processing plant could smuggle out enough plutonium in his lunch box to make a bomb. Although the AEC now requires [*sic*] the screening of the employees with radioactive detectors, the officials said the screening process is normally abandoned during periodic emergency evacuation drills.

Anyone with such thoughts on his mind, it seems, would merely have to wait for such a drill, and the plutonium could be easily taken out.

The *Times* reported further that the spokesman for the AEC had said that there had been seven occasions in the last two years when Government agencies had received plutonium bomb threats. Although they were "believed to have been the work of cranks," an FBI spokesman said that several of these threats were still under investigation.

Regarding the quantity of missing nuclear materials, the *Times* noted that the AEC had reversed its own initial decision and would not now answer the newspaper's questions on the subject. But it reported that experts in processing nuclear fuels, universities, and the AEC itself had made the following allegations: A high official in the AEC had said that one of its plants was unable to account for 9,000 pounds of highly enriched uranium. Controls in another plant were so bad that it would be impossible to estimate the amount of highly enriched uranium that could not be accounted for during the plant's lifetime. Another scientist, with the AEC for many years, confirmed that plants have a cumulative MUF (missing and unaccounted for) measuring in tons. An executive of the Kerr-McGee Corporation, a nuclear power facility said that in 1973 there had been times when the technicians had been unable to account for up to sixty pounds of plutonium. The AEC promptly denied it had ever known this. However, its files revealed that its investigators had repeatedly reproached Kerr-McGee for the way it kept track of special nuclear materials. Its files also showed that Kerr-McGee was closed down on at least two separate occasions in 1974 in an effort to determine how much of the missing plutonium might be in the machinery. An official of Kerr-McGee, who asked not to be identified, said that the plant had been closed down also in 1972 when unable to find approximately fifty pounds of plutonium.

The *Times* article referred back to an AEC special study in April, 1974, by Dr. David Rosenbaum, a consultant on terrorist activity, which had concluded that the potential horror from terrorist nuclear bombs was far greater than from any possible power plant accident. He had projected the possibility of terrorists exploding a bomb in such a critical location as New York City's World Trade Center (which seems to be the favorite spot in most scenarios). A "classified" appendix to the report (the fact that it was classified clearly meant nothing, since it was being published in the *Times*) spelled out a number of methods that might be successful to smuggle out large amounts of special nuclear materials from various specific plants. Such scenarios are termed "black-padding." Other members of the special study group were from such authoritative bodies as the AEC, the FBI, and MIT.

The report sought to buttress its conclusions by again referring back to "three" recent GAO reports. (Prior to this date, supposedly there were only two GAO reports.) The GAO report of October 16, 1974, stated that it had completed a preliminary survey of security measures at nine nuclear plants. "At several . . . we noted unlighted protected-area perimeters, unlocked outside doors, lack of intrusion alarms, and unarmed watchmen." It pointed out that processed plutonium is in small pellets, the size of an eraser on a pencil. It further pointed out that although plutonium is one of the most poisonous materials known to man, a potential smuggler would be safe if the metal did not touch an open wound or reach his lungs. Highly enriched uranium, on the contrary, presents no danger whatsoever to the smuggler.

Significantly, the *Times* article reported that "although the AEC had steadily increased what it calls the 'safeguard' regulations that nuclear plants are supposed to follow, the industry as a whole had resisted tightened security, apparently because of the impact on profits." For example, "The Forum," a nuclear industry lobbying group, quotes Kerr-McGee as saying that the AEC's proposals (scandalously minimal) were "unrealistic and unnecessarily stringent."

Officials of the AEC gave differing estimates of the dimensions of the problem. Manning Huntzing, Director of Regulation, wrote: "It is believed that the problem of safeguarding plutonium is not as difficult as containing the problem of heroin." (That, unfortunately, does not offer too much hope.)

Another commissioner, William E. Kriegsman, told a news conference (September 18, 1974) that "while our safeguard system cannot absolutely eliminate the risk, we are absolutely certain we have reduced the risk to an acceptable level."

But Dr. Charles E. Thornton, a longtime AEC employee, disagreed in a 1972 memo: "Existing U.S. systems for safeguarding special nuclear materials in the custody of private citizens and corporations are incapable of providing assurance that such materials cannot be converted to unauthorized uses." Many experts in such companies as Kerr-McGee, the *Times* reported, did not believe there had been any substantial improvements since then. The *Times* went on to quote another scientist, who refused to be identified, as saying "up until the rules changed last year, the rules were not very strong. And the rules they finally came out with are relatively worthless." It quoted also an unnamed Kerr-McGee official (a firm with one of the most notorious records of missing materials): "We desperately need a system that can quickly detect diversion." With present AEC detection techniques, it "could take as much as six or seven months to discover the diversion of ten or twenty kilograms of plutonium." (A kilogram equals 2.2 pounds.)

The *Times* article mentioned that the situation would become far more serious as plants began using "mixed oxide fuel," uranium enriched with plutonium. The estimate is 100,000 pounds by 1990, and double that by 1995. As bad as the security and bookkeeping were at Kerr-McGee, it was pointed out that other plants had even worse security. And again, in the interest of the public's right to know, the *Times* dutifully listed those plants. (One can only hope that terrorists do not read *The New York Times*.)

Four days later (January 2, 1975) the AEC released a statement in response to the article in the Sunday *Times*. Under the heading "U.S. Says Lost Plutonium Is 'Only a Small Amount' " the AEC insisted that only a small amount was missing from Kerr-McGee and reaffirmed an earlier decision not to answer questions from the *Times* in regard to *how much* was missing from Kerr-McGee and approximately fifteen other facilities in the United States.

By now the *Times* had taken up the position of Taylor. It stated:

> Though some Government agencies have said that a terrorist group could fashion a nuclear bomb with only forty pounds of enriched uranium or twelve pounds of plutonium, one knowledgeable expert — Theodore B. Taylor, an AEC scientist — believes that much smaller amounts of special nuclear materials would be sufficient.

The *Times* went on to describe the comments made by the AEC in response to its article. In regard to Kerr-McGee, "only a small amount is missing," but no comment was made on Kerr-McGee's statement about the missing sixty pounds the previous year. In regard to the report that two Government employees had smuggled out plutonium, "no such instances have occurred." In regard to one plant being unable to account for 9,000 pounds of enriched uranium: "A major enfraction" of all the material processed by the plant "was low enriched uranium which could not be used for weapons purposes."

The AEC concluded by assuring the nation that all was well:

> The commission wishes to emphasize that strict security procedures are in force at all plants which handle significant quantities of plutonium and highly enriched uranium. In

recognition of the increase in acts of sabotage and terrorism in society today — and the fact that the uses of nuclear materials are growing — the AEC has had a major effort underway to strengthen procedures for protecting nuclear materials in the fuel cycle nuclear power program and transportation.

Symbolically representative of those "strict security procedures" was giving old men on retirement jobs .38-caliber pistols.

2. A Media Event: "The Plutonium Connection"

PERHAPS the most significant event in alerting the public to the dangers of nuclear terrorism — and the terrorist to its possibilities — was a media event: the "Nova" PBS-TV show, "The Plutonium Connection." As is usual with PBS, the show was repeated several times on several channels throughout the nation.

TV Guide, in advance of the show, heralded it with a major article written by John McPhee, who was described as "the author of *The Curve of Binding Energy: A Journey into the Awesome and Alarming World of Theodore B. Taylor*." McPhee, in contrast to his earlier condescending remarks, now stated alarmingly:

> Plutonium as an explosive material is superior in several respects to uranium. A piece of plutonium the size of a fist could hollow out the center of a city. . . . That is what India did — using plutonium in a "peaceful" reactor. Every power-reactor now working in the world is steadily making plutonium. In Argentina, in Pakistan, and Japan. In Germany. In Italy. In twenty-five countries. In the United States in particular, plutonium is vulnerable to theft. . . . Who could

make one? A nation — obviously. Any nation. A group of terrorists? Certainly. One person, working alone at home? People who have designed atomic bombs for the Federal Government say yes. Upwards of 10,000 people in the world have the necessary knowledge. One of them is Theodore B. Taylor, a theoretical physicist who has worried about the safeguarding of weapons-grade nuclear materials ever since he learned how comparatively easy a bomb is to design. . . . Some of his bombs were, in their time, the smallest and lightest ever built. They could fit into a paper bag. . . . In the course of preparing documentary treatment of this subject, John Angier, a writer-producer-director for *Nova*, not only talked extensively with Taylor — he also commissioned an MIT undergraduate to research and design a nuclear bomb, working entirely on his own and using only declassified documents that are publicly available. When the student, after five weeks, turned in his design, Angier sent it by prearrangement to Sweden's Ministry of Defense and asked if the bomb would work. The Ministry answered that question on *Nova*.

The TV critic of the *Times*, John J. O'Connor, headed his review with a pun, "Plutonium Connection Proves a Dud." At one and the same time he managed to downplay it, and cite its danger in regard to terrorists watching it. He began by questioning:

At what point does a detailed warning become a primer on the very subject it is supposedly warning against? . . . The primer in this case involves the possible do-it-yourself building of an atom bomb or at least a "crude fission device" that might prove of interest to terrorists in New York, London, Belfast, Tel Aviv, or any other point of current tension. For demonstration purposes, the program assigned a chemistry student, with no previous knowledge of nuclear power, to develop a "practicable" design for an atom bomb within a period of five weeks. A young, bearded man is seen working alone and using only information available to the general public. . . . The student explains how he has acquired declassified Los Alamos data available in books costing five dollars each. The point is simply "how easy it is to build a nuclear bomb." The student outlines the basic design; a central core of plutonium, surrounded by an iron "tamper," then covered with a shell of TNT. With one and a half ounces of plutonium, the device could set off an explosion equal to a thousand tons of TNT. "Boom!" said the smiling student, "you got a bomb — really, it's that simple." The student's design was sent to a Stockholm scientist, an expert in atomic energy, for verification, and the blueprint was judged workable. He also termed the accomplishment "shocking." At this point, even the most casual viewer might wonder about WGBH's intention. Indeed, the program suddenly strikes a note of eerie cautiousness. As the camera pulls away from a closeup of some technical information, the narrator, Robert Redford, explains that the figures are being blocked out "in order not to provide a short-cut for anybody watching." But anybody watching had already been provided with a detailed long-cut.

O'Connor even felt it necessary to warn the reader that PBS-TV was not really compiling a handbook for terrorists. On the contrary, "armed with an imposing roster of experts, scientific and otherwise, the program warns of 'intolerable' nuclear violence by the end of this century." However, he again punned, "the program is not effective; it misfires."

At the outset of the show Taylor noted that he had brought this to the attention of the Pentagon ten years before, in 1965. It rejected his contention as absurd. Therefore, to prove his case, he published *Nuclear Theft*, which provided precise details as to how it could be done. The student who constructed the plans for PBS said that Taylor's book was not indispensable, but it was enormously convenient because it brought together in one source all the necessary information.

The student had begun by using his own college science library, in which the references were "not difficult to find." He worked alone without any expert assistance. He used the book from the Manhattan Project, since declassified, which contained all the information necessary to construct a bomb. His "favorite" was the Los Alamos primer. It was used to orient scientists in the basic theories and fundamentals of bomb design. He described it as "really good for an overview about the theory of bomb design." All the books are available from the National Technical Information Service in Washington, D.C., at about five dollars a book. He got the reference numbers from Taylor's book. The student, surprised that it was so easy to design a bomb, kept thinking, he said, that there had to be more to it than this. But there wasn't. He then described in some detail how easy it is. The Swedish Defense Ministry concluded that there was a good chance that it would go off. Taylor then describes what could happen if such a minimal bomb went off in a busy city. It would kill fifty or one hundred thousand people, not counting the casualties from the resultant panic. It would, "Nova" said, inevitably be the most terrifying blackmail weapon ever devised. And that terrifying weapon can be constructed by an undergraduate chemistry major within five weeks.

The question then posed is why such information is so easily available. One answer is that the information necessary for the construction of a bomb is the same as that used in peaceful atomic projects. And that information has been widely published in numerous scientific journals since 1955 and the "atoms for peace" plan.

To build a bomb you need plutonium. And to get plutonium you have to understand the nuclear fuel cycle. "Nova" then explained that cycle. General Gillen, in charge of security, stated that in the event of a threat you would have to assume that the bomb would go off. Therefore, he said, emphasis should be placed on preventing the loss of plutonium. "Nova" then described the security, or, more properly, the absence of security, at one of the major plants of the United States, Kerr-McGee.

One method is inventory control. But one scientist at Oakridge, Tennessee, stated that with the proliferation of nuclear power plants, it will be beyond the capacity of inventory control to determine whether enough plutonium is missing to construct a bomb. In detail he described the various inadequacies of the measuring system. No instrument can measure it with absolute accuracy. The statistics of the accounting system also have a finite limit. Every two months they are required to produce a full inventory of the plutonium they have handled. The result is a MUF (missing and unaccounted for). A MUF of at least 1 per cent is considered unavoidable. That would amount to the loss of several critical masses in a month. And in that time a bomb-maker could have his project finished. The scientist warned that that is "just not good enough." Another problem, he explained, is that someone might be removing material in a very subtle way. It could take months or years to discover the loss. This diversion of small amounts over a long period is the most difficult type of loss to discover.

Another problem is the technicians themselves in charge of the measuring instruments. The sophisticated people in the system, he stressed, could cause almost complete havoc if they so desired. Another scientist at Los Alamos also discussed the problems of measurement. There are jungles of pipe, rubber gloves, and floor sweepings, which may or may not contain the missing plutonium. Some plants, he pointed out, have sent in containers of plutonium that were 30 per cent inaccurate in their measurement. One proposed solution has been to develop a highly sophisticated computerized system of measurement. But as that same scientist points out, human beings are going to be administering those computers and programming them. They can make the computer lie, very easily. The system can only be as good as the people working for it, he concluded. No system in itself is absolute. There is always some way to work around it.

Therefore, we must rely on trustworthy people who work for it.

"Nova" then dealt with another problem. Simply breaking in, it stated, is obviously the easiest way for a bombmaker to get his plutonium. Again they used Kerr-McGee as an example. It had all the fences, guards, etc., that the AEC required. They had a metal detector for guns, and an explosives detector inside. The objective of any break-in would be the vault, which contains over 400 pounds of plutonium at a time. The whole system, the narrator notes, is designed to keep out maybe one or two thieves. But what size attack should they expect, he asks. He then describes some of the large, well-organized terrorist organizations, such as those in Belfast and the Middle East. In Los Angeles dozens of police were needed to hold down just six members of the SLA. Anywhere terrorist groups have chosen to operate, tremendous opposing forces have had to be brought in. And terrorist groups have repeatedly shown themselves utterly unconcerned about casualties. At Munich they penetrated with ease a conventional security screen surrounding the Olympic Village. Previous security systems, as the Director of Security at Oakridge, Tennessee, pointed out, were designed to prevent espionage, not to repel attacks by terrorists. The guards at Oakridge, a Government weapons factory, are armed merely with pistols.

But if the defenses are not adequate at a Government weapons plant, then what must they be like at the civilian nuclear plants? The director of security at the new Allied Chemical plant has said they are not in a position to repel a significant armed attack. His definition of a significant armed attack was ridiculously low: anything above two or three people.

Similarly, the Atomic Energy Commission has stated that it would expect an attack of between ten or twelve people as probably the maximum threat credible in the

U.S. The civilian plant spokesman boasted, however, that they had communications lines with local law enforcement agencies and military forces. "Nova" checked that out and found that there were only four policemen nearby, and the South Carolina police said they would need forty-five minutes to assembly any significant force. The Kerr-McGee plant depended upon the same reinforcement system. A maximum of thirteen police are within ten minutes away, and large-scale reinforcements, fifty minutes.

Another security gap in the fuel cycle is the plutonium that has to be transported. The approved AEC method of shipment is by commercial armored car of the same type used to carry money. One car carries enough plutonium for two or three bombs. The latest ("increasingly stringent") AEC regulations specify a chase car with two armed guards. Most shipments are arranged by one commercial Washington shipping agent, whose spokesman said there is no question that when special nuclear materials are in the shipment stage, they are most susceptible to diversion. The main problem is overt hijacking. One security measure specified by the AEC is to require communication with the base every two hours. Some of these calls must be made by commercial pay phones; others are made by conventional radio-telephone. There are times when the radio-telephone cannot be used. They run into blackout areas due to terrain. Hijacked in a blackout area, it could be hours before the alarm went out. No one, "Nova" reported, disputes the fact that nuclear transport is insecure.

One proposed solution upon which they were relying heavily is the use of trucks that are supposed to keep people from getting inside for several hours. But that could be easily circumvented merely by hijacking the entire truck. Another aid would be the use of a camper vehicle with a sophisticated communications system, designed to work anywhere, anytime. The basis is the same as the fixed site theory — delay the attack and call for reinforcements, if they are available.

Taylor, asked about the overall response since he first revealed his fears about homemade atom bombs, gloomily concluded: "As of today, we still have quite a distance to go in this country." And since the plutonium security developed in the United States is probably the most advanced in the world (outside Israel and the Communist nations, he should have added), conditions elsewhere make it much easier to divert. As the spokesman for the Swedish Defense Ministry pointed out, security measures in one country are worthless because the terrorist can go to another country where they are virtually nonexistent, get the material there, and then return to the first country.

"Nova" consequently dealt with the measures being taken by the International Atomic Energy Agency, an agency of the United Nations, that now faces an incredible task of keeping track of the world's growing mountain of plutonium. They have materials accounting systems similar to those in the United States. Taylor estimates that there will be over 100,000 pounds of plutonium accumulated in the world by 1980. That gives an idea of their difficulties. It is enough for 10,000 homemade bombs. "Nova" neglects to mention the problem of security within IAEA. We are, presumably, expected to assume that these people are all trustworthy, no matter what nations they may come from. The IAEA relies basically on accounts provided by individual nations. They have to hope that those nations will not tell lies.

Secondarily, they rely on a series of inspections of various plants in these nations. The nation could easily be diverting its own fuel, reprocessing it into bombs. But those visits are made only with the permission of the individual nation and only to certain plants. In fact, the agency only hopes to detect large-scale national diversion, not small-scale, which would be enough for a terrorist bomb. If the IAEA does discover a large-scale national diversion, then, as the head of that agency related, they go through a long bureaucratic procedure of reports to various higher boards, and ultimately to the Security Council of the United Nations. All that would mean is that the world might know about it. But the Security Council would not be able to take any effective action. The inspections are also limited only to those nations that have signed the Nuclear Nonproliferation Act of 1977. That excludes India, Israel, and at least eight other nations. "Nova" concluded that preventing nuclear proliferation is now impossible. Taylor said he thought that by the end of the century there is a very good chance that the use of nuclear weapons, not by national military forces, would have reached the level that most of us would consider to be intolerable. But in the United States, we should note, reactor plant accidents are still seen as the major danger.

They point out that the demand by society that atom bombs do not get into anyone's hands is going to be almost hysterical. And the response to that hysterical demand will mean that everyone involved in the process will necessarily be subject to stringent security evaluations and surveillance, because everyone is a possibility. There will have to be extensive personnel security checks, "reminiscent of the 1950s." There will have to be private dossiers built up, based on answers to such questions as what magazines do you read and whom do you associate with. People will have to be evaluated as to whether they are unstable, and otherwise irresponsible or unreliable. If this is the largest industry, and it is subject to this sort of security, that means the largest fraction of the workers in the nation will be subject to this sort of security. And this, Taylor says, means a garrison state.

"Nova" was unsure whether the garrison state would be

a necessity. What is certain, they said, is that the type of information available to the public will have to be cut back. That, however, seems rather like trying to squeeze the toothpaste back into the tube. That information, as of now, is readily available at the AEC reading room in Washington and in all sorts of widely circulated publications, even popular novels. The AEC (now known by its new name, Nuclear Regulatory Commission) is, as "Nova" said, the first place that the prospective terrorist would go. On file and freely available are the plans of every civilian nuclear installation in the nation. One can examine the layout of the security fences, find out where the vault is inside the plant and the design of its door. "Nova" then quoted Ralph Nader as saying, "It is technological insanity run amok," a vast invasion of privacy, an intrusion of the national security state into most areas of the country where most people live. "Nova" neglected to mention that much of this information was made available due to the agitation of Ralph Nader and others, especially through the so-called Freedom of Information law.

Most important, Taylor points out that it would not do any good to stop the development of nuclear power plants in this nation. The presures would continue in such areas as Japan, which has no indigenous sources of fossil fuels. It is, he says, "whistling in the wind" to call for an international moratorium on the development of nuclear power. While nuclear power plant accidents have to do with the malfunction of machinery, terrorist bombs have to do with the malfunctioning of human beings. We have, Taylor says, a very few years to get this problem under international control. Either we do much more than we are doing today, or even planning to do today, or else within the next five years or so the problem will be cumulatively out of control. By then so much material will have been accumulated throughout the world that to try to put it under heavy safeguards at that point will be impossible.

But since that warning was issued almost nothing has been done. And the minimal things that have been done have in fact made the situation worse, because they have misled the public and elected officials not directly concerned with the problem into believing that all is well.

3. The Debate Gains Momentum

LESS than two weeks after the televising of the "Nova" show the *Times* reported that the Nuclear Regulatory Commission (the reorganized replacement of the AEC) permitted two shipments of approximately a hundred pounds of plutonium to be flown into New York City's Kennedy Airport. The plutonium involved had been produced at an Italian reactor, refined in a Belgian factory, and after arrival at Kennedy was shipped by truck to a Westinghouse factory in Cheswick, Pennsylvania. During a long part of that cycle it was subject to diversion. The *Times* noted that at least two experiments, one conducted by the Federal Government, have shown that persons using publicly available information could build a homemade nuclear bomb if they obtained a small amount of plutonium. The publicity from the article apparently caused the NRC to stop issuing licenses to import and export plutonium, pending a review of the commission's regulations and procedures in this area.

In May, 1975, the NRC announced a decision to delay for three years a ruling on whether plutonium can be used as a fuel for reactors. The decision was denounced by industry spokesmen and the Atomic Industrial Forum (a lobbying agent). The old AEC staff had said in August, 1974, that it should be approved, and that it should resolve later any question about the protection of the plutonium. The *Times* described that decision in May as the first major decision of the new NRC. Yet only the previous month it had run a brief two-inch report on page 15 of its April 19 issue (a Saturday, incidentally, a lax day for readers) that

> The Nuclear Regulatory Agency approved today the export of 1.1 million pounds of natural uranium for processing in Britain and the Soviet Union. The fuel will be sent to West Germany after upgrading at processing plants first in Britain and then in the Soviet Union, the federal agency said in a brief statement. No further details were given. Enriched uranium can yield plutonium as a waste product, the raw material in atomic bombs. The agency has said that it imposed strict safeguards and monitoring regulations over export of uranium to prevent misuse of fuels for military uses.

For the *Times* that evidently was not a major decision. It is intriguing, too, to speculate how the NRC can claim to impose strict monitoring procedures on the Soviet Union.

On June 20, 1975, the *Times* again described how sixty-seven U.N. inspectors were pursuing "lost" nuclear material. The IAEA's inspectors, it said, rely on the collaboration of governments, since they have no enforcement powers. Its head, a Swiss scientist, was reported as not believing in the probability of free-lance nuclear blackmail.

At about the same time the Leonard Davis Institute of International Relations at the Hebrew University in Jerusalem sponsored a symposium on "Terrorism, Preemption, and Surprise." Its conclusions were very different: The technological vulnerability of modern society had made terrorism more feasible and more profitable at less risk to the terrorist. It concluded further that the development of portable, destructive weapons has opened up the options of terrorists. More frightening was the possibility, noted by several participants, that a terrorist group may soon be able to lay its hands on a nuclear device and use it to threaten whole countries. Citing the proliferating of so-called tactical nuclear weapons and absence or laxity of security conditions under which they are often kept, they concluded that a dedicated group could conceivably conceal such a weapon from an army arsenal, or assemble one from plutonium stolen from nuclear plants throughout the world. It also noted the trend around the world for greater tolerance for acts of terrorism and general leniency in the punishment of terrorists, which can be explained partly by a "worldwide societal tendency to place more and more value on human life." Professor George H. Quester of Cornell University points out that this is the thinking behind widespread abolition of the death penalty and, similarly, for a tendency to give into the demands of terrorists when the lives of hostages are threatened.

On September 29, 1975, *U.S. News and World Report* published an interview with Robert A. Fearey, Special Assistant to Secretary of State and Coordinator for the President's Committee to Combat Terrorism. Fearey stated that terrorists do not have any trouble at all in getting weapons. All sorts of small, portable, easy-to-operate, highly accurate and highly destructive weapons now used by the armed forces are in constant danger of falling into the hands of terrorists. He admitted that the U.S. had already had nuclear threats, although none were anything more than hoaxes. "There is no evidence they ever came close to possessing nuclear weapons." Questioned then about homemade chemical and biological weapons, a poisoning of water systems and that sort of operation, he admitted that the possibility of terrorist threats based on such weapons exists: "If one lets one's imagination run, a member of frightening opportunities for terrorists suggest themselves."

By October, 1975, the National Council of Churches and Margaret Mead had discovered the plutonium problem. At its semiannual meeting the Council issued a statement in phrases rather reminiscent of "The Plutonium Connection." It stated its categorical opposition to large-scale future use of plutonium in nuclear power plants as "morally indefensible and technically objectionable." Margaret Mead described plutonium as a "terribly dangerous substance," and said that the United States would have to turn itself into a "garrison state" in order to protect itself against accidental escape of biologically toxic plutonium or its theft by terrorists seeking to fashion nuclear weapons. "It is still possible to turn back," Dr. Mead said, disagreeing with the conclusions of Dr. Taylor, who had stressed that it is irrelevant what the United States does, since the technology as well as the materials are now widely available throughout the world. Evidently it would require a superworld government to enforce a program of further development.

By now the great tax-exempt foundations were taking up the matter. In October, 1975, the Sixteenth Strategy for Peace Conference report, sponsored by the Stanley Foundation, discussed the question of nuclear theft and terrorism. That particular discussion group report was chaired by Dr. Taylor. The report states:

> We considered five possibilities, which we ranked in order of their potential consequences: 1. Theft of nuclear weapons from military stockpiles or production facilities. 2. Theft of nuclear materials from military or civilian programs for the purpose of clandestine construction of nuclear explosives. 3. Theft of plutonium for radioactivity dispersal. 4. Sabotage of nuclear power plants or nuclear waste storage facilities to release enough radioactive materials to be a serious threat to populated areas. 5. Theft of nuclear materials for sale to a black market, or extortion, but not for explicit destructive use.

By 1976 it was clear that a wealth of material had been presented to the public about the potential dangers of terrorism and nuclear weapons. It was, then, strange to find certain experts still discounting the threats. One example that bears citing at length is the article on the Op-Ed page of the *Times* on January 3, 1976, by Richard Wilson, a specialist on nuclear safety and a professor of physics at Harvard. His article basically ignores the plutonium problem, even though he is, as he indicates, aware of it.

"One major problem of the nuclear age", he wrote, "is how to prevent crazy people from making and exploding nuclear bombs." The problem, of course, is not crazy people; it is committed terrorists, who have rather different values than does Professor Wilson, who, like the *Times* itself, considers terrorists to be "insane" or "senseless." He continues:

> Recently, on a television program, a bright student said he had designed a bomb in five weeks. That does not mean that it will work or that he will make one by himself. Moreover, there are other places in society where he can create havoc more easily. [Professor Wilson is in evident disagreement with the Swedish Defense Ministry.] . . . Enough silver cyanide electroplating solution can be put in the water supply to poison an entire city. [Professor Wilson is thus conveniently supplying potential terrorists with a very powerful weapon.] . . . Nerve gas or biological weapons are simple to make. Botulin toxin is much more toxic than plutonium. But a group of a dozen skilled people could make a nuclear bomb when pure materials are available. . . . Until the number of bombs is reduced by disarmament, stealing from the military is a bigger hazard than stealing from civilian nuclear-power sources.

But, as we noted earlier, military bases are at least heavily guarded. Civilian and government nuclear power plants are not. Wilson contends that most American power reactors do not contain enough U-235 pure enough to make a bomb. He ignores the plutonium problem. He does, however, take account of what would be available to a wealthy terrorist group, of which there are several now operating in the world. (Exxon, for example, in 1974 paid over 14 million dollars in ransom to a group in Argentina. One counter-terrorist expert, who contracts his services to corporations, revealed that a West German supermarket chain set the record in early 1977 when it handed over $65 million in return for one of its executives.)

> High-powered lasers are being developed for many industrial processes, and uranium separation with lasers might cost a million dollars and fit into a terrorist's garage. Control of high-powered lasers will therefore be necessary, and it is clear that uranium, not plutonium, is the most dangerous of the nuclear materials.

From this it would seem Wilson still has hopes that plutonium will not, at least in the near future, be used for nuclear fuel. In the meantime, he says, we must develop a good system for safeguarding the plutonium between the time it is purified and the time it is once more in a reactor and again radioactive. He maintains, in opposition to other scientists already cited, that a secure system can be devised that can detect theft in progress and delay it long enough for adequate forces to arrive at the scene. Special trucks can be used for transportation; in a recent test, he exults, it took sixteen hours to open a truck after a simulated hijacking. However, as we observed earlier, there is nothing to prevent the hijacking of the entire truck, rather than merely opening it. Significantly, he reminds us that Taylor had estimated that 100 million dollars would be enough for a system that would be effective against all "credible" thefts, a sum less than a million dollars per power station. The Lincoln Center for the Performing Arts, he pointed out, budgets $850,000 a year for security. Should we not, he asked, spend as much for nuclear power security as an example to the world? But Wilson still conveniently ignored the problem that results from other nations possessing both the technology and the plutonium.

At about the same time a book by Edward Hyams, *Terrorists and Terrorism*, was published. The most remarkable thing about this work is that it manifested a shift in establishment views about terrorism. Prior to this point terrorism had been almost unanimously condemned by the academic elite. Now it was being justified. An extract from Hyams's book was published in the Sunday edition of *Newsday*. We do not suggest that *Newsday* approved the argument. However, what *Newsday* did was to give Hyams a vast audience. Terrorism, he argues, is not ineffectual; if often succeeds. He then attempted, rather erroneously, to enlist in support of terrorism the ethical principles of St. Thomas and John Locke among others. He concluded:

> It seems to me that in the right conditions a campaign of terrorism can succeed in changing the course of history in the sense desired by the terrorists. As a general rule, moreover, that change of direction has been towards a greater measure of social justice for those championed by the terrorists. . . . Can terrorism be justified by success in a good cause? Terrorism is a manifestation of social war and is at least as justifiable as power wars between nations. Objections to the use of terrorism in however good a cause is taken to mean: the property and persons of innocent and unengaged bystanders are injured; women, children, and noncombatant men going peacefully about their business are killed. These consequences of terrorism are horrible and, accordingly, they horrify. But the victims of terrorism are in precisely the same case as the unengaged victims of such "just" wars as World War II; they are sacrificed to men's passion to be free of oppression. . . . Injustice being, as I have said, intolerable, the

"right" of minorities [blacks in the U.S.?] and still more
clearly of majorities [blacks in Southern Africa?] to have a
last resort to violence as a means of redressing their wrongs
has to be conceded; in any case it cannot, in practice, be
prevented except temporarily by means of preemptive police
terrorism.

One wonders if Hyams would be so enthusiastic about the
justification of terrorism if it were he or his family who
were incinerated with a homemade nuclear device.

Hyams's views on terrorism were all the more significant in the light of news reports on January 12, 1976, that
the NRC would assure Congress that week that the threat
of terrorist attacks on atomic reactors and other nuclear
facilities do not justify the creation of a special Federal
security force. At the very same time the *Times*
summarized several recent studies demonstrating that

a band of well-informed terrorists might be able to fashion a
homemade atomic bomb should they obtain a few pounds of
plutonium. The material is also a lethal cause of lung cancer
and could cause widespread delayed damage if it is dispersed
in the air-conditioning system of a large building or in the
atmosphere of a congested area such as Wall Street. A study
by the BDM Corporation of Virginia on the "Analysis of
Terrorist Threats to the Commercial Nuclear Industry"
found that from 1966 to 1975 there were at least twenty-one
incidents where some individuals or a group attacked a nuclear facility.

Despite this, the study concluded that a major attack on
a nuclear site would tax the skill of the most professional
and highly trained commando unit! "Very few illegal action organizations have the organization, training, or
level of skill necessary to carry out a major attack on a
nuclear site." That statement, on the basis of what we
have already presented, is patently false. Even were it

true, it would still be quite chilling, since it tacitly admits that a "few" such groups do have the qualifications necessary to the task. As opposed to Taylor and several other studies, the BDM Corporation report insisted that "no assaults of any consequence had occurred on any nuclear facility due to the absence of motivation, and that no evidence was found to support the contention that present groups have the resources to handle nuclear materials and to fabricate a dispersal device for nuclear weapons." To this the *Times* added that several Government officials maintained that on balance a new Federal force would appear to create more problems than it would solve.

Congressional investigators testified on January 30 that there was no available evidence that international controls had prevented nations from transferring nuclear materials for their power reactors to military programs to construct atomic bombs. An official of the GAO testified that U.S. and international officials had "generally conceded that a country could circumvent safeguards if it was willing to assume the risk of detection, incur the expense, and take the trouble to do so." He called attention to the fact that the IAEA had only forty inspectors to keep track of nuclear materials in the 400 nuclear facilities it is *permitted* to inspect around the world. He warned that "there is no public evidence to show whether agency safeguards have prevented or detected diversion of nuclear materials from intended peaceful purposes. The mere fact that the agency has never disclosed a diversion is not sufficient for many countries that safeguards are effective." He stressed that one reason for uncertainty about the agency's performance is that under international agreements it is prohibited from disclosing results on the grounds that proprietary information might be disclosed.

On the same date the Associated Press disclosed that the U.S. and six other nuclear powers had agreed on the principles governing the export of nuclear power stations. Under the guidelines, recipients must promise not to use newly acquired knowledge to make nuclear weapons. "Promises" are now evidently serving as strict security regulations.

On February 2 *U.S. News and World Report* reported that "the fear of nuclear terrorism is growing among U.S. officials. One expert in domestic intelligence predicts that 'a terrorist group will set off a nuclear weapon sometime in the world during the next five years.' " Increasing concern was being expressed that the next target to be chosen for terrorist attack could be the vulnerable offshore oil- and gas-production platforms that are a major energy source.

Almost simultaneously, in January David E. Lilienthal, first chairman of the Atomic Energy Commission, had urged the halt of further U.S. exports of nuclear reactors. He cited the "terrifying" spread of nuclear fuel and technology that could give scores of nations the atomic bomb.

On February 16, 1976, *U.S. News and World Report* again described several aspects of the problem. One growing concern was that an enemy agent, by sabotaging a power plant, could cause the release of lethal doses of radioactivity into the surrounding air and water. A study made for the NRC by the Mitre Corporation, a think-tank engaged principally in contract work for the U.S. Government, concluded that far tighter precautions are needed. The report spelled out just how terrorists might get their hands on atomic material, including this possibility:

> Organized crime in the United States has demonstrated the capacity to execute complicated actions with planning, coordination, secrecy, patience, and whatever level of force and armament is necessary to accomplish the job. . . . There is no question that for a sufficient amount of money, members of

organized crime would take a contract to acquire special nuclear materials for another party.

One member of the Mitre study team had emphatically concluded: "The safeguards are a joke. The companies involved are interested mostly in saving money. They are doing only the bare minimum of security required by the Nuclear Regulatory Commission." Revealing that even within the NRC there is worry that today's safeguards are inadequate, it quoted an internal memorandum by the NRC's Director of Safeguards, Carl H. Builder: "I am concerned that some or even many of our currently licensed facilities may not have safeguards which are adequate against the *lowest* levels of terrorists' attack." The article noted that the NRC was studying the plutonium recycle questions, but that no final decision was expected for at least a year.

On February 28 the *Times* again described the deplorable safety conditions for nuclear materials and the pathetically ineffectual remedies being considered. Current Federal standards for protecting facilities that handle nuclear materials capable of being turned into homemade bombs were well below the maximum threat Government nuclear experts believe such facilities could face. The "maximum threat" itself was, it should be remembered, preposterously low. The situation had prompted the Nuclear Regulatory Commission to *consider* the need for increasing guards and other security measures at nuclear facilities.

The government's present standards require that facilities handling highly enriched uranium and plutonium be capable of repulsing an attack by two terrorists and delaying an attack by up to ten. But a draft report prepared last November by the Commission's staff found that most experts believed that a terrorist gang attacking a nuclear facility would probably involve up to twelve persons.

The *Times* then erroneously stated that the threat pos-
tulated in existing Government standards was disclosed
only today. Quoting a transcript of testimony by Kenneth
R. Chapman, Director of the Commission's Office of Nuclear Safety and Safeguards, it said that the current security system is based on "a threat that provides for
guards at the site to effectively overcome two aggressors
and to withstand for certain periods of time larger numbers of aggressors until local police or other law enforcement agencies can respond." As noted earlier, that usually
involves several *hours*.

Chapman further disclosed that the guards at the nuclear facilities were armed only with pistols and shotguns
and that the standards assumed the aggressors would
have only "small arms." That statement was especially
ludicrous, since at the same time the Pentagon was disclosing that there had occurred large numbers of thefts of
quite sophisticated weapons from Federal bases and arsenals. The *Times* article — conveniently for would-be terrorists — listed the sixteen facilities in ten states that are
licensed to handle large amounts of special nuclear materials. It further quoted Mr. Chapman as having testified
that "there had been no instances of armed attacks on
licensed nuclear facilities in the United States. There
have been a number of acts of sabotage here, however, and
during the last two years there have been two terrorist
attacks by an unknown number of persons on reactors in
France and one by more than ten persons in Argentina. A
bomb was set off during one of the French attacks."

The article cited a November study by the NRC, which
had examined nineteen relevant studies and conducted
interviews with analysts from the FBI, the intelligence
community, the Department of Defense, and state and
local law enforcement agencies. "What emerged from
this," the *Times* reported, "was a consensus estimate that
an external threat group would probably number about

six to eight people and very likely will not exceed twelve persons." (No basis is ever given for arriving at such a small number in a terrorist group.) But the Mitre report, concluded in September, disagreed. That study, headed by Dr. David Rosenbaum and composed of a team of security experts, stated: "Our estimate of the maximum credible threats to any facility or element of transportation handling special nuclear materials is fifteen highly trained men, no more than three of whom work within the facility or transportation company from which the material is to be taken." The Mitre report also raised serious questions about the Commission's present assumption that terrorists attacking a nuclear facility have only small arms. And well might they have questioned that statement. Back in September the Pentagon had disclosed that during the past three years sufficient weapons, ammunition, and explosives to outfit ten combat battalions had disappeared from United States Army installations. They were defined as small arms and ammunition. But the Pentagon's definition of small arms and ammunition varies considerably from the NRC's definition. The Pentagon, by "small arms," means automatic weapons (machine guns, for example). By "small arms" the NRC means pistols and shotguns.

On March 1 *U.S. News and World Report* in a major article reported that

> losses from U.S. bases worldwide include rifles, pistols, grenade launchers, and even surface-to-air missiles and anti-tank rockets. In January a 70-pound live shell was taken from a Navy weapons depot and left on a deserted street in Oakland, California. A note with the shell said the theft was made to demonstrate how easily arms can be stolen. Defense officials insist that so far no U.S. nuclear weapons had been stolen. But guards at sites where nuclear arms are stored have had to ward off trespassers. On several occasions, shots were fired into the air to frighten away prowlers.... Conven-

tional ammunition may be disappearing faster yet — at the rate of one million or more rounds a year. Defense security officials say they have no reliable estimate because of a lack of precise record keeping. . . . Police have found caches of military weapons in Boston and elsewhere in recent years. At least a portion of military losses have been picked up by terrorists. Various weapons identified by serial number as belonging to the U.S. Armed Forces have been taken away from at least two terrorist groups — the Baader-Meinhof Group in West Germany and the self-named Japanese Red Army. The Irish Republican Army . . . is regarded as a major customer for illegal U.S. military arms.

Describing one theft from a National Guard armory in Texas in November, in which M-17 rifles and grenade launchers were taken, the article continued:

The sophistication of the break-in was as much a matter of concern to investigators as the losses. Among other subtle touches an alarm cable was short-circuited without sounding, and a special padlock, thought invulnerable, was broken. The padlock was found in fragments, leading investigators to suspect it had been first frozen with a liquid-nitrogen spray, then shattered with a hammer blow. U.S. bases overseas report similar losses. . . . Pentagon officials complain that many of the thefts occur through the cooperation of soldiers and civilian employes who have access to weapons.

The magnitude of the losses caused Representative F. Edward Hébert and others in Congress to question base security techniques.

But the great fear, the article went on to stress, is "that terrorists not only can get their hands on the more conventional weapons but may succeed eventually in capturing a nuclear explosive. The U.S. has thousands stored around the world, in all shapes, forms, and fire power." It quoted Joseph J. Liebling, top security officer of the Pentagon, as saying "the loss of even one nuclear weapon would be catastrophic." The article also reported that this year alone the Pentagon would spend 42 million dollars to improve the protection of several hundred major weapons depots. That sum, of course, is less than half of what the Pentagon had said they needed the previous year. But it would take at least two years, Defense officials say, to get all improvements in place. So far, Defense officials acknowledge, they have failed to come up with a plan that would halt the thefts completely. In fact, the Pentagon security experts are resigned to continued thefts. The sheer size of the job of overseeing the installations is a major reason. According to Mr. Liebling, who has been dealing with security matters at the Pentagon for the past thirty-five years, "it is impossible to cut the thefts altogether. We can only hope that losses will continue to decline." Congressman Hébert, who was not known as a Pentagon-baiter, also sardonically observed that the Pentagon often tries to wipe out the loss of 450 guns as a bookkeeping mistake.

On March 18 the Associated Press reported that Federal officials had disclosed that there have been at least 175 actual instances or threats of violence against nuclear facilities, mostly power plants, across the nation since 1969.

On March 26 Senator Ribicoff, in an article on the Op-Ed page of the *Times* warned:

> The potential for a holocaust-producing showdown between the superpowers is the most immediate nuclear danger, but the greater danger may lie in the spread of the nuclear weapons to many nations, even to terrorists, due to the export of civilian nuclear technology. . . . Today, the refusal of France and West Germany to restrict their civilian nuclear exports poses the greatest obstacle to curbing dangerous nuclear trade.

On the very same day it was widely reported in the media that the Ford Administration had announced a new approach to terrorism. The Cabinet-level committee dealing with the problem was headed by Henry Kissinger. According to the *Times*, "the new approach to the terrorist problem emerged at the close of a confidential two-day conference on international terrorism sponsored by the State Department, which drew almost two hundred specialists from four countries." (It seems rather silly to have kept it confidential if its results were going to be released to the press.) "There is going to be a big change," an official said, "but we haven't decided yet whether to do it over a period of four or five months or over a period of a year." State Department officials said that the proposals under study would include emergency teams of psychiatrists and police specialists familiar with what is termed "coercive bargaining" in situations involving terrorists. It was reported that the State Department office, under Robert A. Fearey, Special Assistant to the Secretary of State and Coordinator for Combatting Terrorism, functioned mainly as a headquarters for information gathering and policy direction. Fearey was to be replaced later that year by a former CIA officer with considerable field and operational experience. The *Times* explained that for the participants in the conference the critical issue on terrorism confronting the Administration "was how to modify the policy of simply refusing to bargain with terrorists." As justification they cited the example of the American Ambassador to Tanzania who successfully bargained with the terrorists who had kidnapped a group of Stanford University researchers. Martha Hutchinson, a political scientist at Wesleyan University, was quoted as a representative view: "I think the American concept is totally inapplicable. I think we need to study the possibility of bargaining with terrorists."

The new approach was directly contrary to the highly successful Israeli policy of refusing to bargain at all with terrorists. It was even more stupid to announce the new policy in the press for the benefit of prospective terrorists. Incredibly, over a year later, two widely recognized "experts," Yonah Alexander (editor of *International Terrorism*) and Dr. Frederick Hacker (author of the much-publicized *Crusaders, Criminals, Crazies*), spent most of their time on a TV show (WOR-TV, N.Y., May 10, 1977) denouncing the U.S. Government for its policy of non-negotiation. One wonders about the quality of advice being provided by such "experts" if they are that uninformed.

On March 30, Congresswatch (Nader's pressure group) made public a response it had received from the NRC. Beyond the threats and instances of violence against nuclear facilities, the Government admitted that there had been twenty-eight threats of violence involving the use of nuclear materials against other targets since 1970. The Commission revealed that since May 4, 1969, there had been ninety-nine threats, break-ins, or other events in facilities operated by private industry. Most were directed at nuclear reactors operated by utilities. The Energy Research and Development Administration listed seventy-six threats or acts of violence in the same period to nuclear facilities owned or operated by the Government. ERDA also said that there had been at least nine arson attempts at the Lawrence Research Laboratory in Berkeley, California. It described how the Government had proposed fining a Pennsylvania utility $8,000 after the company security force failed to apprehend a mentally ill former employee who had entered the protected area around the utility's nuclear reactor. The fine against the Metropolitan Edison Company was the sixteenth such penalty imposed by the NRC for inadequate security around a nuclear facility in two years. A fine of $8,000, however, is hardly an adequate incentive to spend money for security.

On April 19 *U.S. News and World Report* disclosed that although "it's rarely acknowledged in Washington . . . there is rising concern in Europe over whether terrorists could lay hands on any of the seven thousand nuclear warheads the U.S. stores at scattered bases. The Pentagon says they are securely guarded. Not all Europeans agree with that optimism." Only a few weeks earlier, as we noted, the Pentagon had reluctantly (and contradictorily) admitted that they were *not* securely guarded. Since the Government tends to deal with nuclear security in terms of years, it seems unlikely it had remedied this problem within a few weeks.

On April 27 the *Times* divulged that "on the day a federal agency publicly said that health problems at an Oklahoma plutonium factory were of little significance, an official in the same agency was privately telling the top executive of the company that the factory had serious problems."

Once again the plant was Kerr-McGee, and the whole matter was related to the rather suspicious death of Karen Silkwood. According to the *Times*, James G. Keppler, regional director of the then AEC, said in the private statement that "there was no evidence that anyone in the Kerr-McGee Corporation outside the plant was concerned about what was going on there; that equipment in the plant was archaic and prone to breakdowns which enhanced contamination problems; and that a large number of errors resulted from such causes as personnel turnover, inadequate training or lack of supervision." It quoted another witness, Dr. Karl V. Morgan, "an enthusiastic supporter of nuclear energy and a leading authority on safety," as saying that "in thirty-four years he had never known an operation in this industry so poorly operated as the Kerr-McGee factory."

Kerr-McGee typically refused to comment on either Mr. Keppler's memorandum or Dr. Morgan's charges that the company failed to follow accepted safety and security practices. But during the long trial that grew out of Karen Silkwood's death (settled finally with very large damages awarded for the plaintiffs in 1979), all that had initially been charged was simply confirmed by several witnesses under oath.

Kerr-McGee based its entire defense on the argument that the employee had herself taken the plutonium out of the plant and intentionally poisoned herself. That defense by the corporation *proves* our point — that an employee can easily take plutonium out of the plant, their "stringent" security precautions notwithstanding.

By this time the whole problem was beginning to filter down to the popular political columnists. C. L. Sulzberger of the *Times*, in a column entitled "Merry Thoughts for May" (1976), pessimistically, but quite accurately, anguished:

> To an increasing degree terrorist movements find it easier to carry on operations in cities rather than by traditional guerrilla warfare. Their usual textbook is the *Mini-manual of the Urban Guerrilla* by the Brazilian revolutionist, Carlos Marighella.... Terrorists, who have already shown how they can use the openness of democratic society to protect themselves, may some day use the terrible developments of modern weaponry to exploit their cause. During United States Congressional hearings about poisons stocked by the Pentagon for possible wartime use, an old theoretical paper was discovered. This pointed out how easy it would be for a few people to ride through the New York subway system dropping off toxic materials and ultimately destroying the city. Moreover, it is now acknowledged as conceivable that terrorists could hijack a nuclear warhead and use it for blackmail or destruction. It is not even beyond the bounds of belief that urban guerrillas, already expert in the home-manufacture of explosives, could some day make atomic devices. This no longer requires immense power supplies or even

a phenomenal scientific genius. Where does such gloomy speculation lead? Certainly not to accords at Geneva to give urban guerrillas the rights of prisoners of war; nor to more marchers behind May Day's Red banner. Rather, as Major Gen. Edward Lansdale, American expert on terrorists, conjectures: "My hunch is that history is waiting to play a deadly joke on us."

On May 11, 1976, Robert Kleiman, a member of the editorial board of the *Times*, described another aspect of Government stupidity:

At a Moscow conference on nuclear proliferation last summer, the scientist who built Russia's first A-bomb in 1949 turned to an American visitor. "Do you know Henry DeWolf Smyth?" he asked, speaking of the Princeton physicist who wrote the official, declassified history that told Americans in 1945 how the United States had made the atomic bomb. "At one international meeting," the Russian said, "I shocked Smyth badly. 'Henry,' I said, 'You helped us very much. Your book was always at my side.' 'Impossible,' Smyth said. 'Everything was in the public domain.' 'Henry, Henry,' I said, 'Everything that had to be done might have been done in several different ways. You told us which path to take. When it didn't work, we knew we had simply made some mistake and started again. Public domain, indeed!'" [See p. 72 on the recent release of Manhattan Project materials.]

That book by Smyth was one of those cited by the student on "The Plutonium Connection". Kleiman concluded that "with terrorist seizure and regional wars possible, the world will be lucky to get through the century without losing a city."

By now the usual people were becoming quite hysterical and proposing their typically unrealistic solutions to the problem. United Press International reported on a study by Denis Hayes, a senior researcher at the private, non-profit Worldwide Institute in Washington, which warned that terrorists in Third World nations are almost certain to convert atomic resources designed for peaceful use into weapons. It consequently called for the "magic sesame" solution of the worldwide abandonment of nuclear power. Hayes said that one study had already suggested that plutonium contamination has spread through the ocean and may have entered the human food chain. But, he said, the far greater threat is that terrorists may pirate nuclear fuel or developing nations may use it to make crude but dangerous atomic weapons. Acceptance of nuclear technology amounts to the virtual certainty that some nuclear bombs will end up in the hands of terrorists. Although already too late to halt entirely the widespread dissemination of the scientific principles underlying nuclear power, what can still be sought is the international renunciation of this technology and the grave threats it entails. Terrorists can steal nuclear materials with relative ease, Hayes said, and build a bomb or blackmail a nation by threatening to scatter highly toxic plutonium dust over a city from a plane. Hayes understates the danger. Something more is known than the mere principles underlying nuclear power. The precise details on how to make bombs are known. And as far as getting all the nations of the world to agree to renounce nuclear power, as we noted before, that is utterly unrealistic. Getting all of the nations of the world to agree on anything would be unrealistic.

In the spring of 1976 four leading American nuclear experts gathered at Princeton University for the televising of a TV show to be broadcast in England. They were: Dr. George Kistiakowsky, Eisenhower's science adviser and a pioneer in nuclear explosives; Dr. George Rathjens, former chief scientist for the Pentagon; Dr. Theodore Taylor, former nuclear weapons designer; and Herbert Scoville, former chief of scientific intelligence at the CIA. All four warned that politically unstable nations or desperate groups of fanatical terrorists will inevitably make and use the atom bomb unless the controls on the use of nuclear power are tightened. Scoville warned: "The risk that a nuclear war will break out is growing day by day. I believe that nuclear war is probable and that it will involve large numbers of deaths. By the year 2,000, fatalities could run to one billion." All four warned of two primary dangers: the irresponsible international trade in nuclear fuel reprocessing plants necessary for fuel enrichment and the production of bombs, and the growing stockpile of plutonium. Taylor stated: "There is the possibility that an aggressive or beleaguered country, or a deranged leader in charge of a national government, might seek a way out of their problems by using the most powerful weapon ever invented." Dr. Rathjens suggested that Israel, Taiwan, and South Africa were possible users.

In late May, 1976, a Federal appeals court in New York barred the use of plutonium commercially until the completion of a thorough study of the safety of the fuel and its effect on health. The most significant aspect of this ban was that the court seemed to be concerned primarily with the problem that the material might fall into the hands of a nation or group that might use it as a weapon.

Two days later, May 29, the NRC ordered a nationwide security alert to all fifty-eight then operative nuclear power plants. It also asked the security forces to make sure that their communications with local law enforcement officials were intact. The NRC spokesman said that this was not the first of such alerts, nor did he expect it to be the last. UPI reported that police sources in Illinois said that extremist groups might try to seize the power stations by June 8. According to the *Times*; "The federal standards for protecting nuclear plants appear to be inadequate to combat the maximum threat that nuclear experts believe such plants face." It went on to describe how two bombs were exploded the previous May 12 at the headquarters of one company. It was followed up by a letter from an organization calling itself the Fred Hampton Unit of the People's Forces. (Hampton was the Black Panther killed in a police raid in Chicago in 1969.) The NRC later disclosed that its nationwide security alert was based on intelligence reports that two groups may have had plans to take over at least one nuclear plant; in addition, eighteen previous threats had been made against individual installations in 1976. It revealed further that the credentials and some other belongings of two of its inspectors had been stolen "and their unauthorized possession created concern that they might be used to test entry of a nuclear facility."

The wire services also reported that a journalist, associated with the FBI, had said there is enough missing plutonium to suggest that a nuclear black market exists in this country. "Official documents I examined," she said, "indicate an exceedingly high figure involving plutonium in excess of that which would be lost in pipes in normal processing. This would lead me to believe in the possibility of nuclear gunrunners dealing in black-market plutonium." The journalist said she had documents that showed the unaccounted-for nuclear material to be in excess of ten times that allowable under NRC guidelines. The charges were denied by the usual sources, and the credibility of the journalist was attacked. But less than a year later the probability of a plutonium black market would be widely acknowledged.

In mid-June *Newsday* published a two-part article by Denis Hayes, an extract from his Worldwatch paper entitled, "Nuclear Power: The Fifth Horseman." Hayes again vehemently argued that dependence upon nuclear power will result in authoritarianism, ecological damage, and terrorism:

Discussions of nuclear terrorism have generally focused on the use of fissile materials to manufacture nuclear weapons, a vitally important topic. But neglected are a motley range of other opportunities for nuclear sabotage and disruption. With careful planning and tight discipline, armed groups could interrupt the fuel cycle at any vulnerable point and escape with fissile material. Perhaps more frightening, however, is the inside thief — the terrorist sympathizer or the person with gambling debts or the victim of blackmail. In 1973, for example, the director of security for the U.S. Atomic Energy Commission was found to have borrowed almost a quarter of a million dollars, to have spent much of it on racing wagers, and to have outstanding debts of $170,000. Quiet diversion of bomb-grade material may have taken place already. There are many documented instances of plutonium being found where it should not have been found, and, worse, not being found where it should have been.

In June a newly declassified CIA study warned that there was a good chance that within the next few years foreign-linked terrorists would be increasingly tempted to stage major actions in this nation. The study attempted to assess the global dynamics of terrorism and was prepared by a CIA analyst who used a comprehensive data bank developed by the Agency. Carrying the disclaimer that it did not represent an official CIA position, the report concluded that even if international accords and tighter security measures are able to prevent some terrorist attacks, nevertheless, within the next few years "we should expect to witness steadily greater and more widespread sophistication in targeting, execution, and weaponry. Such weapons might include nuclear bombs."

Another dimension of the problem emerged in June 1976. The media reported that the Ford Administration's chief arms control official had set off a controversy between two Government agencies by accusing three American scientists of injudiciously publishing sensitive information on nuclear technology. What such scientists may have uppermost in their minds, of course, is promotion and the possibility of Nobel and other prizes. According to the *Times*: "The incident also served to highlight a recurring dilemma, according to knowledgeable officials — the desire to foster the dissemination of advanced scientific knowledge as opposed to the need to protect information that is sensitive to national security." The accusation was made June 15 in a speech in Miami by Fred C. Iklé, director of the Arms Control and Disarmament Agency, who said he was "disturbed" by recent cases of publication of a new technique for enriching uranium, and that "spreading information about this technique could make it easier for other nations to circumvent our controls against nuclear proliferation." He did not specify either the new techniques or the names of the scientists.

Other Administration officials disclosed that he was referring to papers by scientists employed by the Los Alamos laboratory. The *Times* then, again no doubt in the interest of comprehensive news coverage, described in some detail what Iklé had refused to disclose about the technique, who the scientists were, and where the papers might be obtained. Immediately after publication of their papers, the *Times* noted, a professor of biochemistry at Harvard raised a cry of protest about what he regarded as a contribution to the potential spread of nuclear arms-making capability. The biochemist replied to the complaint by saying that this was a "hot" scientific field in which even Soviet scientists were publishing a good deal. In defending the declassification, Dr. Seamans, head of the Energy Research and Development Administration, said: "There was sufficient information in the public domain not to classify the papers." (In this connection, compare the comments above of Robert Kleiman on how such declassifications aided the Soviets.)

On the same date the media reported that the Government was for the first time developing a disaster plan to cope with the casualties, property damage, and loss of civil control that would be caused by a serious accident at one of the nation's nuclear reactors or by an explosion of a homemade atomic bomb by a terrorist group. The draft of the plan, leaked to the *Times,* predicted that with the growing use of nuclear energy across the world the potential for such peacetime nuclear emergencies will continue to grow.

On July 18 *Newsday* reported that the limited international conventions on terrorism already in force — The Hague Convention of 1970 and the Montreal Convention of 1971, which ban only aerial piracy — had proven ineffective. For one thing, not all nations signed. For another, a signature is hardly enough. One of the signatories of the Montreal Convention was Uganda, whose officials reportedly aided the Palestinian hijackers. *Newsday* continued:

> And while the nations of the world continue demonstrating their inability to agree on means of stopping international terrorism, the threat grows. Experts such as André Pierre of the Council on Foreign Relations contend that the proliferation of nuclear power plants will allow terrorists to obtain materials for nuclear weapons. Others say that the lack of firm measures against terrorists simply encourages more terrorism.

On August 6 the GAO issued a report stating that the U.S. could not account for over two tons of atomic bomb material. That MUF concerned only Government nuclear facilities; it did not include civilian nuclear facilities. The report had been requested a year and a half earlier by Representative John D. Dingell (D. Mich.) after the *Times* had reported that Government and industry facilities together were unable to account for thousands of pounds of special nuclear material.

According to four officials with access to the classified study, the GAO found that over the years the thirty-four Government facilities operated by what is now the Energy Research and Development Administration were unable to account for more than 100,000 pounds of what the technicians call special nuclear material. Only 6 to 7 per cent of this total, according to the Government, could be easily fashioned into weapons. This would mean that the Government is unable to find at least 6,000 pounds of material of weapons grade. The *Times* quoted an earlier statement by Dingell to the effect that only 36 pounds of enriched uranium, or 13 pounds of plutonium, were required to make a nuclear weapon.

On August 9 *U.S. News and World Report* reported that although the threat of nuclear war through the 1980's is discounted, nuclear terrorism is viewed as a growing threat and "the real danger." The article quoted an unidentified intensive study of the problem by Government analysts, which concluded: "It is the 'psychotic, anarchical groups,' whose behavior is entirely unpredictable, that pose the real danger when it comes to nuclear blackmail," and that the more established terrorist groups, such as the PLO, would be unlikely to use nuclear blackmail because of adverse effects on world public opinion. (These were essentially the conclusions reached in a special report issued by the Institute for the Study of Conflict in May, 1975, and also in several German studies, as reported in *The German Tribune*.) A nuclear arms specialist on the panel was quoted as saying that "the only thing that gives you some feeling of serenity is that it is still not all that easy to acquire a nuclear weapon, move it secretly and use it. And the groups that have the greatest ability to do it are precisely the ones that have the least motive to do it." That statement ignores the problem of a group constructing its own nuclear weapon with stolen plutonium.

The study concluded that it would be more likely for a terrorist group to seize a nuclear power facility and threaten to pollute a city with radioactive material. The panel's scientific expert pointed to a much more likely and much easier threat: "If your aim is to blackmail a government or to establish the seriousness of your purpose, it's a lot easier to use chemical and biological contaminants. These are easier for terrorists to acquire, easier to move secretly, and easier to use in a controlled way than nuclear weapons." (They are, however, somewhat less spectacular.) The overall danger of a nuclear weapon being detonated in the years ahead by a terrorist or a criminal gang was summed up by the panel's arms analyst: "It's like Russian roulette. But instead of six chambers in the gun, there are perhaps 100 chambers. So maybe we can get by." Small comfort, in the judgment of many experts.

On August 5, 1976, the eve of the anniversary of the bombing of Hiroshima, the TV show referred to earlier was shown on PBS-TV in New York. It was entitled "The Nuclear Question." As well as anything, a review by Leo Selgsohn in *Newsday* summed up what had been done thus far in the matter of providing security to prevent nuclear materials from being stolen, and the prospects for the future. His review is worth quoting at length.

It was not a highly promoted show, nor widely viewed by commercial-TV standards. . . . But of all the TV shows I've seen in the past year, it is the only one least likely to go away. It was not the 1945 horror footage of Hiroshima victims that had the greatest impact, but the final, almost banal, filmed statement of four atomic-energy experts that was the most compelling and chilling part of the evening. . . . The four men were the antitheses of everything that makes for good TV. They were dull scientists delivering their little speeches in the weary tones of men who have said it all before and didn't expect anyone to listen. They sat stiffly at a table and sounded almost bored. Yet it was precisely this sterile, TV-verité ambiance that set off their words so starkly. I realized that here was TV's ultimate horror show. They were saying that doomsday is probably just around the corner, that a thermal nuclear holocaust before the end of the century is "probable." These were no Doctor Strangeloves or pop alarm-

ists. This was an all-star cast of some of the most knowledgeable men in the world. . . . Here were voices in the
wilderness delivering their unthinkable litany late in the
night over a public-television station. . . . The horror projected from that screen was that they had all but given up.
The evidence piled up like the sound of muffled drums: the
once-great secret of making a thermal nuclear bomb is now
no secret at all; a handful of terrorists would not find it
difficult to steal the essential plutonium, make a bomb and
hold a city hostage; nations great and small, stable and unstable, are busy building thermal nuclear plants, increasing
their capacity to devastate in wartime by design or peacetime by accident. Nuclear-control agreements are hardly
worth the paper they are written on. . . . In terms of the
millions who watch TV, WNET/13 made hardly a ripple with
its doomsday special, except in the minds of those who
watched it. It will be hard to forget.

In September, 1976, a British Royal Commission
warned of the "entirely credible possibility that terrorists
could seize material to build a [nuclear] bomb." The same
month *Newsday* reported that

Yugoslav officials reportedly let Carlos, the notorious international terrorist, believed the mastermind of the 1975
Vienna kidnapping of Arab oil ministers, slip through their
fingers last week, and the United States is angry about the
fumble. State Department officials said yesterday that they
gave the Yugoslav government full details about Carlos'
whereabouts last week.... A Cairo newspaper reported yesterday that Carlos... is loose in Europe with a small nuclear
bomb which he apparently intends to use in a terrorist operation.

In late October, 1976, the AP provided an update on
those "stringent" security measures being taken at nuclear sites in the United States. It said that armored
personnel carriers and guards equipped with the army's

latest rapid-fire rifles were being added to the security forces at fourteen Federal nuclear sites. Nothing was said about increased guards at the civilian sites. It further reported that guards at one site were now under orders to "shoot to kill" in situations involving theft or sabotage of nuclear weapons. The spokesman for the NRC said that the upgrading was begun after the GAO study had recommended it because of increasing terrorist activity. According to the AP article: "Officials at the Hanford Nuclear Reservation . . . said yesterday that 32 additional guards were in training there. The guards, already equipped with shotguns, side arms, and M-14 automatic rifles, are now getting flak jackets, helmets, gas masks, and the M-16 rifles. The Hanford guards also will get two of the machine-gun-equipped armored personnel carriers." An ERDA official said that the 10 per cent increase in guard force was about half complete and would continue, along with weapons upgrading, into 1978. He declined to list the number of new guards being assigned to installations other than Hanford, saying "that had not been decided in some cases."

Thus, after four years of repeated warnings by experts in various fields, the Federal Government has managed to provide only these minimal, indeed trivial, safeguards.

4. Plus ça change, plus c'est la même chose

IT WAS divulged in December, 1976, that the U.S. Government had lost track through sloppy bookkeeping of "sizable quantities of weapons-grade" nuclear materials leased to foreign nations in the 1950's and 1960's. Asked how much was still unaccounted for, an Arms Control and Disarmament Agency official replied: "I consider it a lot." Under international agreements such materials are supposed to remain under American control. "But if we don't know how much it is or where it is, we obviously cannot control its use," the official commented. It seems that about a year earlier it had occurred to officials that the weapons-grade nuclear materials could be turned into atomic weapons, the official recalled. The agency requested the information from ERDA, which replied that the only readily available information was from 1968 on. Asked again for information prior to that time, ERDA replied that it had neither the resources nor the urge to collate the data from the old handwritten ledgers of the AEC. Only after much badgering from the Arms Control and Disarmament Agency and on appeal to the head of ERDA did it begin to send them photocopies.

On the matter of safeguards, the Associated Press reported in late 1976 on the latest "increasingly stringent" precautions being taken — not at all plants, but at only fourteen Federal nuclear sites. ERDA proudly announced that armored personnel carriers and guards equipped with the Army's latest rapid-fire rifles were being added to the security forces at these sites. It said too that guards at the Nevada Test Site had orders to shoot to kill in situations involving theft or sabotage of nuclear weapons at the bomb-testing facility. That statement seems to indicate that prior to then the guards were not allowed to shoot to kill someone stealing a nuclear weapon or sabotaging the facility and thereby releasing deadly radioactivity.

To rely on personnel carriers and rapid-fire rifles as safeguards against the arms currently available on the international arms market (centered according to several reports in Amsterdam) or the sophisticated weapons being stolen in large quantities from U.S. armories and bases seems ludicrous. The moves were, however, described by ERDA as part of "a little-publicized" buildup of security forces at research centers, test sites, and production facilities that had begun three years ago after a GAO study had recommended it because of increasing terrorist activity. ERDA was once again assuring the Republic that it was right on top of things. But, as we have demonstrated at some length, no such program had *begun* three years ago. Only certain rather minimal proposed changes were put forward for discussion, and, at that, generally resisted by all parties involved.

In concrete terms, we find that the "increased security" announced in 1976 is alarmingly inadequate. The upgrading, according to ERDA's assistant director for policy and planning, Earle Hightower, would replace their .38-cal. revolvers with M-16 rifles (which are not as good as the ones being used years ago by the Viet Cong) and would provide for all of the sites twenty-seven surplus armored personnel carriers armed with M-60 .30-cal. machine guns, i.e., about two each. The site getting the largest increase in guards, Hanford Nuclear Reservation in Richland, Wash., would receive thirty-two guards, or about ten per shift for a vast reservation. Guards there, ERDA boasted, would also receive flak jackets, helmets, and gas masks. Overall, there was to be a 10 per cent increase in the guard force by 1978.

In early February it was prominently reported in all elements of the media that a Princeton undergraduate had designed an atomic bomb, and that various nations, including France and Pakistan, were beating a path to his door in hopes of purchasing the plans. The materials, he reported, would cost a mere $2,000. It had taken him five and a half months to complete the design from information available in the college library and publicly available Government papers he had obtained through the mail and during a visit to Washington. FBI agents, evidently not having seen "The Plutonium Connection," were described as amazed, and completely unaware that this could be done. The student, of course, then began making the

rounds on the "talk" shows. For example, on New York's
WNEW-TV's "Midday Live" the Princeton student appeared with his design for a nuclear bomb and was greeted
as if he had just taken first prize at the local science fair.
Since the student also had a flourishing, entrepreneurial
pizza business on campus, host Bill Boggs seemed uncertain which enterprise to probe first for exciting details.
After learning that mushroom pizza (no pun intended)
was the most popular, along with other interesting facets
of campus pizza business, the politically "consciousness-
raised" host interviewed his student-guest on his bomb, as
if the whole thing had not been done before. The entire
spectacle seemed to confirm Marx's morose observation
that if history is tragedy the first time around, the second
time it is farce.

The NRC finally announced on February 19, 1977, after
a year-long study, that it had concluded that the possible
threat of terrorist actions, whether theft or sabotage,
against the nation's seventy-four civilian-operated nuclear facilities required an "immediate and significant
increase in security." In a fifty-seven-page unclassified
version of a report on terrorist dangers it listed the steps to
be completed in six months. To the NRC half a year is
"immediate," it seems. And what it regards as a "significant" increase in security follows: full field background
investigations for selected employees; arming the guards
with semiautomatic rifles; increasing the number of
guards; and explaining to them their duties and responsibilities. Again the report took note of the "considerable
reluctance" of the civilian nuclear industry to accept any
increase in security. It cited the industry's position that
this level of threat should be a Federal responsibility and
that the necessary levels of defense would be damaging to
company images.

Reportedly, the key decision made by the NRC was that
the facilities must be safeguarded against threats involv-

ing "two or more" persons inside the facility acting in concert with an outside group of terrorists using automatic rifles, recoilless cannons, and plastic explosives. The NRC had believed until then — incredibly — that the maximum credible threat would be from one employee and three outsiders armed with pistols and rifles that could be obtained legally. Upping the estimate from one to two or more inside and from three to a group outside was described as the "basic change" that led to the decision to require "major strengthening of security." Continuing to downplay the situation, the NRC said that in the absence of specific threats emergency measures were unwarranted. In short, wait until it happens before we do anything that might be effective.

On the same day, ironically, the State of California distributed a thirty-page handbook outlining procedures to be used by local governments in dealing with threats of nuclear extortion. It urged local communities to "think the unthinkable." Advising on how they may be able to determine whether the terrorist or extortionist actually has a nuclear device, the handbook significantly stopped short of giving any advice on what to do if they were convinced the threat was valid. One high security official explained that if the community is a small rural one, it might decide to evacuate; but if it is a major city, it would probably have no alternative but to give in to the demands. At the same time Los Angeles officials disclosed that there had been a nuclear threat in an attempt to extort money from a major industrial company within the past eighteen months. Federal and local authorities established an ad hoc committee of law enforcement and technical experts to deal with it before they eventually decided it was a hoax. In response to media questions Mayor Beame of New York said that that city had no special plans for dealing with nuclear threats. But it did have, he assured the public, a special hostage-negotiating squad.

A day later an NRC director admitted that some reactors are protected by as few as three guards at any one time. Warning that new requirements would double or triple security costs, he nevertheless said they were "prudent" of the worldwide increase in terrorism. These major increases in security, he related, would give the guards "more powerful" weapons (semiautomatic rifles) and increase their number from three to ten on one shift within ninety days.

A week later, February 28, 1977, in conjunction with a discussion about the revelation of a threat of mass (chemical) terrorism in New York City, the *Daily News* there reported that the NRC had only that week ordered all plants to "tighten security" against possible terrorist attacks. "Armed guards," the *Daily News* stressed, would have their numbers "greatly increased under the new Federal order," and "they already patrol the Indian Point tract" of Consolidated Edison. From three ill-trained men to nine is now being described as "greatly increased" by the nation's largest newspaper in its work of keeping the public well informed. A spokesman for Con Ed, the *Daily News* reported, "declined to discuss the security system because, he said, 'if you talk about security, it's no longer necessary.'" Directly contrary to the statement by Mayor Beame regarding California's handbook for dealing with nuclear threats by terrorists, Police Commissioner Codd insisted that his department had contingency plans for all kinds of disasters.

The same day the West German Government disclosed that one of its most prominent nuclear physicists, Dr. Klaus R. Traube, had had frequent contacts with several internationally sought terrorists over a period of at least six months during 1975-76. Traube had access to all blueprints for nuclear power plants in West Germany. "He could have given instructions," the Minister of Interior said, "for attacks from the outside as well as for penetration by terrorists, and unleashed the potential dangers of nuclear energy against the public." Fearing that nightmare, the Minister had authorized a break-in and planting of a bug in Traube's home. That action was, of course, vociferously denounced by the media in Germany as an illegal and flagrant violation of privacy and civil liberties. The terrorists with whom Traube was associating had been responsible, among other actions, for the kidnapping of the OPEC oil ministers, several attempts to bomb nuclear plants in France, and the Entebbe hijacking.

On March 2, 1977, the National Advisory Committee on Criminal Justice Standards and Goals issued a 661-page report warning that the danger of high technology terrorism is so great that every state should have the power to pass legislation rapidly to deal with emergency situations. The part of the report dealing with technological terrorism was based on a study by R. W. Mengel of the BDM corporation in Virginia. He too concluded that it is now possible for terrorists with "reasonable resources and talent" to make an atomic weapon. Even the immediate fatalities, he estimated, would be in excess of 100,000, and the damage would total in the billions.

Meanwhile, the U.S. Government was busily engaged in declassifying yet more documents to make the whole thing even easier. Thirty-five volumes, including technical data, on the Manhattan Project were declassified after a thirty-year waiting period and are now publicly available at the National Archives. The papers were extracted by two historians into a single volume they hoped would become a best seller.

In April, 1977, the GAO issued yet another report attacking security in nuclear power plants. It described the security as so loose that they might be unable to hold off an attack by even the most ill-equipped saboteurs. It placed the blame for the situation directly on the NRC. It pointed out that the new regulations to upgrade security by 1978 left far too many areas unprotected until that time and should be supplemented with "immediate interim measures." An NRC official disputed the conclusion that it was moving too slowly, but accepted most of the other points. According to the GAO, "the greatest single shortcoming of power plant security is the quality of the guard forces," with some recruits being given as little as four hours' training before beginning work. One wonders, however, whether it is the judgment of the GAO that giving the guards semiautomatic rifles and increasing their number from three to ten will provide adequate security in years to come.

In April the AP reported that Federal officials had admitted that plutonium was still being shipped by air over the western United States. The Colorado Health Department complained that in the event of an accident the radioactive material "could contaminate large populated areas." An easily obtained SAM rocket could help the accident along.

In late April the Union of Concerned Scientists (a group opposing atomic power plants) obtained more than 50,000 documents under the "Freedom of Information Act." The documents cast doubt on the veracity of the NRC. They showed that the NRC's report that the plants were safe contained numerous omissions, flaws, deletions of strong criticisms from staff members, such as the likelihood of sabotage or other terrorist action, which the Union described as a "glaring deficiency." The chairman of the AEC at the time the report was issued was James R. Schlesinger.

Earlier the same month, April 4, 1977, James H. Conran, a security analyst with the NRC, sent an eight-page letter to President Carter, the three sitting NRC commissioners, and Representative Udall (who heads the House Subcommittee on Energy and the Environment). That letter concisely and clearly substantiated the main thrust of this work, that in regard to the problem of nuclear safeguards there has been an utter lack of any effective response. *The New York Times* obtained a leaked copy of the letter and published its main points on May 25, 1977. During two years' work on the security of weapons-grade materials, Conran said, he had concluded that "existing safeguards are afflicted pervasively by serious and chronic weaknesses which pose serious potential hazard to the public health and safety, and which even appear to threaten (potentially, at least) the national security." Also that NRC and ERDA officials had deliberately suppressed specific information needed by other Government officials (especially the security agencies) and the public to make decisions about protecting nuclear materials. The information the NRC and ERDA had denied to other Government analysts dealt with how easy it would be for a terrorist group to make a nuclear bomb, the credibility and implication of extortion attempts that had already occurred, and "serious indications that a successful diversion of a large quantity of special nuclear material from at least one existing processing facility might already have occurred at some time in the past." Conran closed his letter to the President by pointing out that he had brought his concerns to the chairman of the NRC well over a year ago, but that the NRC's response had been inadequate.

The response to Conran's letter was predictably typical, characteristic of what has been occurring since 1965, when Taylor made known his concerns. The chairman of a special seven-man panel established to evaluate the charges, while admitting that several had "technical merit," said that the panel did not agree with his main conclusion that the weaknesses in the safeguard systems posed serious hazards to public health and national security. He denied as well that the NRC had engaged in deliberate and systematic suppression within the Government of information relating to vital nuclear security issues. Since the special panel's report was then at the National Security Council undergoing classification review, he refused to divulge any information contained in it. The *Times* went through its by now pro forma statement that the NRC had made several recent moves to tighten security at the plants, neglecting to specify just what those "increasingly stringent precautions were."

About two months after the disclosure of the content of James H. Conran's letter and the Government's initial response, the *Times* reported (July 25, 1977) that on June 30 the NRC had in fact "formally adopted an 8-point action plan" based on his allegations. The Commission had also pledged that it would "work to insure that its public statements about the special nuclear materials accurately describe the circumstances, the remedial action taken, and the resolution of the problem." A day later, in testimony before a Senate Committee, Conran charged that the Government files contained "disturbing indications" of successful attempts to damage nuclear facilities and to steal nuclear materials that could be fashioned into homemade atomic weapons. Earlier he had alluded to a "large amount of special nuclear material" that "might have been stolen from the processing plant in Apollo (Pennsylvania)," and now he spoke of evidence in the Government's files of "malevolent actions or interest directly against nuclear facilities, or to the theft and misuse of special nuclear material, in a continuing and even increasing manner." The Commission, he concluded, had not successfully confronted the problem concerning the theft of special nuclear materials.

But, between Conran's letter of April 4 and the NRC's announcement of July 25, 1977, a number of important disclosures about safeguard deficiencies at nuclear plants and for nuclear materials in transit had surfaced in the news media. Two of these — about the possible theft in 1965 of 381.6 pounds of highly enriched uranium that could not be accounted for in Apollo, Pennsylvania (which may have become the "target," as the new report said, of international thieves"), the other about a possible "diversion" by Israel of 200 tons of uranium that disappeared from a freighter in November, 1968 — will serve as our point of departure in the following chapter. Here we want to note merely an international sharpening of awareness, in the spring of 1977, that a crisis was in the making in the sphere of nuclear safeguards.

In mid-May, 1977, the International Atomic Energy Conference met in Salzburg, Austria. At a news conference there the Director of Safeguards of Euratom, the EEC's nuclear group, emphasized that international "safeguards" cannot prevent incidents such as the 1968 diversion of a shipment of uranium to Israel. "The diversion," he said, "was detected when the ship did not arrive. The community (EEC) had no legal means of containing the affair." It is, then, as simple as that for a bandit nation or a terrorist group to obtain the weapons-grade materials.

One of the major themes of the conference was nuclear safeguards. Walter Sullivan, who reported on it for the *Times* (May 22, 1977), summed up the problem and the conference's conclusion:

> In a world that has people desperate enough to blow up airliners, mow down bystanders in an airline terminal, or abduct high officials for ransom, how can explosive nuclear materials be safeguarded against theft? ... Countermeasures discussed were national, directed against thefts by terrorists, and international, directed against governmental diversion to gain nuclear weapons. On both levels it was agreed that no system can be foolproof.

Rudolf Rometsch, head of the safeguards program for the IAEA, gave some indication of his problems to the conference. That year, he said, IAEA inspectors would have to visit sixty facilities. In ten years there would be several hundred; and in twenty years, thousands.

Much reliance was being placed on computers by the experts attending the conference, completely unaware, evidently, of what the computer security experts were saying, that is, that computers themselves lack any effective safeguards and can be quite easily compromised. In a discussion of other protective measures Richard T. Kennedy of the NRC (responsible for safeguards in commercial facilities) and Harvey E. Lyon of the ERDA (responsible for safeguards in Government facilities) both warned that the insider who can neutralize the operation of the protection system is "a severe threat." They and other experts stressed the value of designing nuclear plants that would facilitate inspection and monitoring. That, we think, may be properly called a "long-range" solution. In any event, those would be technological safeguards. And as Rometsch dolefully observed, "if technological safeguards are the only protection, the system can be beaten." It is, in short, a problem of "people" security.

5. Prometheus, Israel, and the Apollo Diversions

IN EARLY April, 1979, the eyes of the world become riveted on Three Mile Island, Pennsylvania, as a nuclear power plant teetered on the edge of radiological catastrophe.

Little is clear at this early time about what actually happened there other than that it was a spectacular illustration of that same syndrome of irresponsible behavior by the corporate officials and the NRC that we have so laboriously documented here. As Dr. George B. Kistiakowsky (professor of chemistry emeritus at Harvard, a pioneer in nuclear explosives and one-time top-level science adviser to President Eisenhower) wrote in a letter to the *Times* (published April 15, 1979) during the crisis:

> I consider this bureaucracy about the most arrogant and contemptuous of public interest among Federal agencies, as manifested by its decades-long fight against the lowering of the radiation exposure standards because making them safer for the workers and public might interfere with the AEC's (and its successors') activities, the decades-long neglect of safety research on nuclear power reactors or radioactive waste disposal, etc., and its ready distortion of facts to fit the agency's position, as in the "executive summary" of the Rasmussen report on reactor safety.

The corporate officials at Three Mile Island repeatedly assured all at the outset that the accident was minor. They continued to do so even after the NRC said the situation was extremely critical. The ideological right, continuing to function as a cat's paw for unrestrained corporate capitalism and labor, insisted that the whole thing was "a local mishap," "a sensationalized media event." Indignantly, such corporate and political spokesmen demanded: "Was anyone killed? Was anyone killed?"

We'll have more to say later about the attitude of the Nuclear Regulatory Commission as evidenced in the transcript subsequently released of the conversations at its meetings during the course of the crisis. But what about the attitude of the ideological right on this whole question of safeguards against theft or sabotage or seizure for terrorist purposes at nuclear plants or against hijackings of nuclear materials in transit? Do the editors of William F. Buckley's *National Review*, for instance, believe that our Government has the moral will or even the "security intelligence" to safeguard our nuclear materials against terrorists or hit teams of what are now called "potential adversaries"?

One might assume, without specific inquiry, that "security-conscious" conservative groups in this country would be of one mind in assessing the gravity of the nation's situation in this sphere. In issue after issue of *National Review* and other publications on the "respectable" right we find hardline declarations that our national security intelligence is now virtually nonexistent. Quite typical are these words of M. Stanton Evans in the July 6, 1979, issue of *National Review*:

> The crippling of U.S. intelligence capabilities has been a major goal of liberal forces in recent years — a goal that they have triumphantly attained. Thanks to a steady drumfire of criticism in the press, congressional exposés, denunciations by defecting agents, and agitprop from Communist sources, the Central Intelligence Agency, along with the FBI and other security agencies, has been effectively throttled. [All of this] has put the intelligence community in shock, and made it afraid to lift a finger in its own behalf. Throughout this orgy of recrimination, the liberal media and liberal forces in the Congress have served as cheering sections for the anti-intelligence crusade. And now . . . the Senate is contemplating further restrictive measures that . . . would bring effective U.S. intelligence efforts to a grinding halt.

If that indictment is true, is it reasonable for security-conscious conservatives to feel confident that our Government is capable of securing our nuclear installations against "penetration" by terrorists or, worse, the highly trained hit-squads of needy friends or determined foes? According to *National Review*'s special issue on nuclear power (February 2, 1979) — titled "Prometheus Bound" and characterized by its editors as "unique in the history of the magazine" — the answer to our question ought to be, apparently, a resounding Yes! Its very title suggests assurances that we have little to fear: the ancient Promethean gift of fire, which man has ingeniously developed into an explosive power capable of reducing our planet to a smouldering ash (*solvet saeclum in favilla*, as the old hymn had prophesied), is not out of control but, rather, safely bound to a cliff. That, at any rate, is the explicit argument of Bernard L. Cohen's featured article, which "demonstrates that nuclear power is both safe and necessary," as also of the companion piece by B. Bruce-Briggs titled "Terror and Anxiety" — an extended review of the books *Nuclear Theft: Risks and Safeguards* by Mason Willrich and Theodore B. Taylor, and *The Curve of Binding Energy* by John McPhee that we discussed earlier. In addition to Cohen and Bruce-Briggs, the editors of the "Prometheus Bound" issue of *National Review* had enlisted the intelligence of fifteen other confident "experts" to deal with related aspects of its theme in ways that support the optimism of its title.

An introductory note explains that the idea of a special issue on nuclear power had grown out of the response to an earlier article by Professor Cohen, "The Case for the Breeder Reactor," in the September 16, 1977, issue of *National Review*. In the earlier article Cohen's avowed purpose was to confront and dismiss any problem of nuclear terrorism; and in the later article too, Professor Cohen stresses:

1. that the needed uranium/plutonium has become increasingly inaccessible to terrorists — "in thirty years, there has never even been a theft attempt, and safeguarding techniques are improving rapidly";
2. that to design a nuclear bomb is far more difficult than procuring the materials, since it "requires reasonable expertise in nuclear reactor physics, hydrodynamics, computation techniques, chemistry, electronics, and high-explosive technology, plus some familiarity with health physics";
3. that to proceed from designing to actually fabricating a device is even more difficult, since it "would require

thousands of dollars' worth of equipment and would take many weeks or months of concerted effort";

4. that even if terrorists could get this far, it wouldn't be worth their while, since, with "all this effort and risk," the most that could be done would be to "kill the occupants of a large building," and there are "many easier ways to accomplish that end."

How much truth is there in Professor Cohen's reassuring assertions that the "possibility of stealing enough plutonium to make a bomb is now very remote" and that there is "no evidence that any significant amount of plutonium was ever diverted for illegal uses"?

We reserve for later our extended discussion of the large quantities of highly enriched uranium that were reported missing and had apparently been "diverted" from the small nuclear facility at Apollo, Pennsylvania. Here we note only that, as if to mock Professor Cohen most directly, during the very week when *National Review*'s "Prometheus Bound" issue was on the newsstands, the AP, the UPI, and *The New York Times* reported significant thefts of plutonium/uranium. AP reported that on February 1, 1979, a worker at General Electric had broken into a 275-pound container of uranium and had stolen 150 pounds as part of an extortion scheme. On February 9 UPI reported that Federal agents were holding two individuals in connection with the seizure of 5,000 pounds of stolen uranium that was apparently on its way to an unidentified buyer in El Paso, Texas, and that, three months before, two 1,000-pound barrels of uranium had been stolen.

All *The New York Times* could report during the week of February 2 was that a Nuclear Regulatory Commission inspector drove through the gate of an upstate New York nuclear power plant without being challenged. But just a month earlier (January 4, 1979) it had reported an official acknowledgment from Washington that "a consignment of nuclear fuel" destined for Roumania had been "tampered with before the shipment left the United States." The report specified that the

> seals placed on four canisters of highly enriched uranium . . . to deter possible efforts to remove the weapons-grade material, had been broken. . . . The Federal officials were said to have replaced the broken seals and to have sent the canisters through to Roumania on Dec. 16 without checking whether any of the enriched uranium had been removed. . . . The incident has set off a dispute in which the State Department aides are complaining about the apparent laxity of the Nuclear Regulatory Commission.

What about the nuclear plants themselves? In his 1979 article Professor Cohen had assured readers of *National Review* that our plutonium stores are safe against terrorist theft, because, in coming out of the heavily guarded storage areas, even "people with special clearance . . . have to pass through monitors which are capable of detecting very small amounts." Again, as if to mock his assurances, in March, 1979, several publications revealed that there was now in circulation a report published by the NRC itself titled *The Barrier Penetration Database*, which gave precise instructions on how to break through sensors, doors, walls, ceilings, or any of thirty-two barriers that an intruder at a nuclear power plant might encounter.

NRC officials hastened to explain that circulation of the report was deemed necessary "to supply the NRC and nuclear power plant licensees with basic data" about what tools intruders would have to have and just how long it would actually take them to break in. Critics of the report contended that it obviously combined all the information any serious terrorists would need. "All the nuclear plants are concerned about this," said Leon Russell, chief engineer at the Calvert Cliffs Nuclear Plant in Baltimore, since "making such information public almost dares certain people to try to break into a power plant." Had it been a mistake to publish the report? No, said Dr. Anthony Fainberg of the Brookhaven National Laboratory, one of its co-authors. "This gives the crazy person a little bit more data than he would otherwise have," Dr. Fainberg acknowledged. "But the overwhelming benefits of allowing the free flow of information more than offset the very minuscule possible risk that is involved in this case." Obviously for Fainberg, as for Dr. Cohen, Prometheus remains securely bound, since only a "crazy person" would want to break in and steal his fire power.

Where are the terrorists who, even if they managed to steal enough plutonium or uranium, would know how to design and actually build a nuclear device? Haven't there been TV and newspaper reports in depth about how first a student from MIT, then one from Princeton, then a third from Harvard had succeeded in designing "workable" bombs, even though they lacked serious technical training and could consult only unclassified books? In his 1979 article Professor Cohen attacks and contemptuously dismisses the idea of student-designed bombs. Moreover, he adds with confidence, "nobody who's ever worked on our atomic bomb project" would presume to say whether "some particular design would or would not work," because he "would be divulging very secret information" in violation of the law.

But Professor Cohen is on all counts wrong on this subject, and he ought to have known it. Less than a year earlier the Senate Subcommittee on Nuclear Proliferation, headed by former astronaut John Glenn, had heard testimony from "a 22-year-old former Harvard student with only one year of college-level physics" about how he had "designed a series of nuclear weapons . . . in the last five months from material that was available to the public and without the help of any government, corporation, or person." According to the *Times* report of March 22, 1978, two scientists with many years of experience in designing atomic weapons had done precisely what Professor Cohen had said such experts would not do: They had told the subcommittee that the young student had done an unusually proficient job, that his design was indeed workable. One of the expert witnesses was Dr. Theodore B. Taylor, who from 1949 to 1956 had been a member of the team designing nuclear weapons at the Los Alamos laboratory in New Mexico — an expert for whom Dr. Cohen professes high respect. The young student's manuscript on the subject, Taylor testified, "is the most extensive and detailed exposition that I have seen outside the classified literature."

According to Senator Glenn, the central fact borne out by the expert testimony at his subcommittee hearings was that initial lack of knowledge of nuclear weapons was no longer a barrier to their manufacture. "In other words," he said, "if the mechanical equipment of the bomb is available, the only lacking ingredient for a truly workable bomb is uranium enriched to weapons grade or plutonium."

But what sort of "expert" is Professor Cohen? Certainly he is not an "expert" bomb-maker, like Dr. Taylor. As he quite candidly acknowledges in his 1979 article: "I personally would not know how to build a nuclear bomb, as I have never been involved in that sort of work." What he presumes to be an expert on is evidently the "mentality" of terrorists and the "uses" to which nuclear terrorism is limited. And in that sort of expertise he is joined by B. Bruce-Briggs, author of the companion piece on "Terror and Anxiety" published in the same "Prometheus Bound" issue of *National Review*.

We noted earlier Cohen's basic argument that terrorists wouldn't build a nuclear bomb even if they could, because all they could do with it is kill the inhabitants of a large building, which they could just as easily do, in his words, by releasing "a poisonous gas in the ventilation system of that building." At least as many people could be killed, with far less trouble than it takes to make a bomb, by using "conventional explosives or incendiaries in large crowds, as at sports stadiums"; or by poisoning "a city's water or food supplies." Any of these measures, Cohen concludes, "would be simpler, safer, cheaper, and faster than stealing plutonium and making a bomb." Ergo, there can be no risk at all that, despite the collapse of our security agencies, terrorists will so much as want to unbind our Prometheus, much less succeed in doing so.

Bruce-Briggs does, however, admit that "a gang of serious terrorists or criminals could knock over a nuclear power or fuel-processing plant facility and obtain fissionable materials." But then he repeats Cohen's arguments that most terrorists wouldn't know what to do with such materials, and that if one of them could conceivably design a bomb, why would he want to "fool with atomic devices, which are easily detected through radiation, when he could kill or threaten multitudes with means more readily at hand — such as, to take the most obvious method, poisoning water supplies?"

The answer to Bruce-Briggs and Cohen lies in the rather obvious fact that the true purpose of terrorism is not to kill people but, quite simply, to *terrorize*. True terrorism is political theater, and its essential imperative is this: You kill some people in order to terrorize those you don't kill. Conventional explosives, however destructive, have ceased to terrorize our generation in any theatrical sense. Putting poison in the ventilation system of a large building can be passed off by a government as some as yet unidentified new virus. And the other chemical and biological options suggested by Bruce-Briggs and Cohen can be similarly passed off. But no nuclear explosion, however small, can be explained away in that fashion. Dr.

Cohen nowhere takes up the question of a credible nuclear-terrorist threat. In its place he prefers to insist, as we have seen, that it is one thing to design a bomb and quite another to fabricate one, since everything is so hard to get and costly to do. Yet, as we have seen, thousands of pounds of plutonium and uranium are in fact currently missing. If the Government at some point receives a threat with sophisticated bomb designs, what then does it do? Does it cave in to the blackmail? Or does it ignore the threat and risk a major disaster?

Perhaps Dr. Cohen might advise us all to join Bruce-Briggs in the comforting assumption that "terrorists are all basically imcompetents." That, Bruce-Briggs says, "is summed up in an Israeli explanation of the miserable performance of the Arab terrorists: 'The Palestinians have good jobs in Kuwait: PLO is the dregs.' . . . terrorism is for losers." Is Bruce-Briggs unaware of the fact that Israel has in the past produced terrorists who were not losers, who were anything but incompetent? Israel has produced them, and so have many other nations, past and present. He comes close to acknowledging this when he seems to warn that, "as Lewis A. Dunn of the Hudson Institute has emphasized, the worst threat to nuclear materials is from commando units or intelligence agents of foreign governments." He here adds a parenthetical remark — "A state friendly to the U.S. is widely believed to have been hijacking already" — but graciously refrains from identifying the friendly and thoroughly competent hijacker. Needless to say — and here we cross over into the sphere of the second focus of our chapter — the state in question is plainly Israel, whose government has a much more realistic sense of the dangers and uses of nuclear terrorism than our own has ever had.

The best-informed opinion seems to be that the State of Israel began hijacking uranium in transit on the high seas some time in the late 1960's. Before that Israel had apparently been able to get uranium out of the U.S. simply by smuggling. But when the smuggling was detected and in large measure stopped, "hijacking and clandestine purchases" proved themselves, apparently, to be viable alternatives.

As it has unraveled itself in the news media, the story of Israel's "extra-legal" efforts to acquire the materials necessary for its physical and psychological security against the potential of Arab technological terrorism begins with a UPI report of May 9, 1977. It is a report that B. Bruce-Briggs may have seen, for it has to do with a case of uranium hijacking at sea. Before UPI ran its story, the London *Observer* had reported the arrest in Norway of a member of an Israeli "hit team" that had allegedly killed eleven Arab terrorists in Europe. The man had been charged with murder; and to escape the penalty for that crime he had evidently plea-bargained with the Norwegian authorities, confessing instead to the lesser crime of having hijacked uranium into Israel many years before.

According to Norwegian authorities, the Israeli hit-team sharpshooter very obviously knew the "whole story" of what had happened in 1968 to a German freighter that had been carrying "enough uranium to build 42 nuclear bombs." In the UPI account we read: "The disappearance of the uranium cargo in 1968 was disclosed April 30 (1977) in a speech by Paul Leventhal, a former counsel to a United States Senate Committee at a nuclear conference in Salzburg, Austria." Israeli agents had been negotiating to purchase the vessel in question and therefore had a purchaser's access to it. Quite inexplicably it disappeared from sight for a while; and then, as Paul Leventhal explained in Salzburg, it turned up again, in a few weeks, "with a new name, a new registry, a new crew, but no uranium." Less than a year later that same Paul Leventhal would publish an entire book on the subject, characterizing the "case of the phantom uranium ship" as "one of the world's best kept secrets," confirmed, as he put it, only to a "select group of nuclear officials, diplomats, and intelligence agents."

But before commenting on that book we have to trace at least in outline the gradual buildup of evidence of thefts or diversion of nuclear materials, not in transit, as in the case of the phantom uranium freighter, but directly from American plants.

On July 4, 1977 — just two months after the phantom uranium-ship hijack disclosures of the London *Observer* and UPI — David Burnham of *The New York Times* began what proved to be an annual series of articles (at least three have appeared each year since the first) on official Government reports concerning "several curious developments" at a small nuclear facility in Apollo, Pennsylvania. Mr. Burnham disclosed, first of all, that the Apollo facility had been cited by Government inspectors for having repeatedly violated basic "safety and security regulations," but that it had nevertheless continued to receive Government contracts worth millions of dollars. In Burnham's words:

> The most serious of the hundreds of violations cited over the last 20 years was a 1965 finding that the facility could not account for 381.6 pounds of highly enriched uranium, enough to serve as raw material for at least 10 nuclear bombs. Government officials have contended that the material was lost in complicated manufacturing processes and was not stolen.

The trouble with that explanation, Burnham went on, is that rigorous General Accounting Office (GAO) inspectors severely discount it and even the Nuclear Regulatory Commission (NRC) doesn't believe it. In June, 1975, the NRC had in fact issued a 90-page summary of the chronic enforcement problems at the Apollo facility. In it we read at one point: "The loss of highly enriched uranium prompted the AEC [Atomic Energy Commission] to question 400 persons and refer the case to the FBI. For reasons that are not clear the FBI decided not to investigate." Upon reviewing the summary, the NRC regional director said: "This obviously was our worst performer." But the founder and first president of the Apollo facility, Zalman A. Shapiro, could be brought to say only: "We operated within the rules and regulations."

Burnham began his chronicle of violations at the Apollo facility with an inspector's report of 1960, which concluded that "the company did not have adequate control over the nuclear material in its possession," and which was followed, in 1964, by "another finding that internal control procedures were inadequate and that the uranium reports being submitted were not complete and factual." On March 23, 1965, the Apollo directors were told that the Government would bill them $2.8 million for 657 pounds of uranium that "could not be found." Burnham dutifully notes here that both the old Atomic Energy Commission and the Nuclear Regulatory Commission that succeeded it "have repeatedly asserted that there was no evidence that the highly enriched uranium had not been obtained by any unauthorized person or nation." But, not less dutifully, he then reviews the General Accounting Office's far less reassuring appraisal of the situation. He writes:

> The GAO said it could not come to a definite conclusion about what had happened to the uranium. The condition of the company records, the summary reported, did not permit the GAO auditors to make a conclusive determination as to the time or the manner in which the losses occurred. An FBI spokesman, in response to an inquiry, declined to comment on why the bureau had chosen not to investigate. Three separate officials familiar with the case, however, reported that the FBI did investigate whether a senior official of the Apollo facility was an agent for a foreign country. The investigation, one official said, found no evidence that he was.

Which senior official? Which foreign country? For specific answers in this regard we have to wait for David Burnham's article of August 4, 1977 — exactly one month after the first. The Government had that very day, Burnham noted, for the very first time published reports with concrete figures on the overall dimension of the problem of nuclear materials currently categorized as MUF (missing or unaccounted for). Unofficial estimates were much higher, but the Government's official report was that 8,000 pounds of highly enriched uranium and plutonium were missing. Again it was specified that the facility at Apollo, Pennsylvania, appeared to be a principal offender with respect to safeguards. Clarifying his remark of a month earlier, Burnham notes that the unaccounted-for "losses" at that facility had led to an investigation by the FBI and a separate investigation by the CIA, to determine whether one of the facility's top executives was an agent of a foreign nation.

Though the AEC had "concluded that there was no evidence of theft," Burnham wrote, "several intelligence officials have said there was widespread speculation that the uranium may have been stolen by agents of another country, specifically Israel." In his follow-up article of August 8, 1977, the *Times*'s specialist on nuclear theft news added a detail saying that, according to a House of Representatives investigator, U.S. intelligence officials had "strong suspicions that highly enriched uranium, the type that could be used in bombs, was stolen from a Pennsylvania nuclear facility more than a decade ago."

Why had the FBI declined to investigate the "strong suspicions" and "widespread speculation" of possible Israeli theft of the materials reported missing at Apollo? On October 18, 1977, the Associated Press reported on evidence that, in 1966, President Johnson very explicitly "told Richard Helms, then director of CIA, not to pursue an investigation of why 400 pounds of bomb-grade uranium was missing from a Pennsylvania fuel plant," even though Helms had said the CIA was convinced uranium had been diverted to Israel. When contacted on October 17, Helms had dutifully refused to discuss the matter; so had the Carter White House a week later, though Press Secretary Jody Powell subsequently told reporters that "four years of continual investigation by the AEC, the FBI, and the GAO all failed to reveal that such diversions did occur." Responding to calls from the *Times*, the Israeli Embassy in Washington reportedly said:

> The wording of Mr. Powell's statement today seemed to indicate that as far as President Carter was concerned the investigations into possible theft from the United States nuclear facilities were now a closed matter and would not be pursued.

The account in the *Times* cautiously explained: "It may be that the Carter Administration, which has had uneasy relations with Israel and its supporters ... does not wish to open another possible source of friction."

A month later both the *Washington Post* and *The New York Times* discussed at length the substance of an article by Howard Kohn and Barbara Newman that had originally appeared in *Rolling Stone* magazine. It alleged that in the late 1960's Israel had uranium from West Germany and France under the cover of staged hijackings. Two real hijackings of uranium apparently occurred in 1968, but then two more were staged with the cooperation of West Germany, who received "full payment," though clandestinely, in cash and scientific information. Cohen and Newman commented that Israel had undertaken the hijackings and clandestine purchases only after it was forced to halt a ten-year smuggling operation that had netted it from 200 to 400 pounds of bomb-grade uranium from the processing plant at Apollo, Pennsylvania. "The stolen material," Kohn and Newman concluded, was of course "used to give Israel a last resort military alternative in the Mideast."

Both the *Post* and the *Times* accounts denied that the Kohn-Newman article had solid evidence to support it. And so did the Israeli Embassy and Defense Secretary Harold Brown, when questioned on November 27, 1977. But by then the *Times* already had in its possession "two classified documents written in 1976" that linked the uranium missing from the Apollo plant with Israel. And, according to David Burnham, other documents, obtained under the Freedom of Information Act, showed that many officials in the old AEC were deeply concerned about the way the president of the Apollo facility, Dr. Shapiro, ran his plant, which employed several alien technicians and often admitted alien visitors. According to Burnham, a secret summary of the case, apparently prepared for President Ford in 1975, contained the following:

Harold Ungar, a Washington lawyer now representing Dr. Shapiro, said his client's position is "very simple: he never diverted a single microgram of nuclear material to Israel or anyone else and does not believe that anyone else did so at the plant." Mr. Ungar also said: "If they're pursuing Dr. Shapiro because he is Jewish and a Zionist, for which he offers no apologies, it's a hell of a basis for an investigation."

The documents used by Burnham were later evaluated by the *Christian Science Monitor* (November 15, 1977) and explored in greater depth. What "the released documents and interviews with several people who ought to know much of what there is to know ... reveal," we read in that issue of *CSM*, "is that the plant in Pennsylvania failed for a considerable period in the 1960's to maintain adequate safeguards and bookkeeping and that the plant's president had, according to a 1963 FBI report, 'very close ties with Israel.' . . . There was a feeling among some congressional sources that people in high places covered something up. But . . . 'the trail is cold,' said one congressional specialist who had studied the matter."

According to one document, the *Christian Science Monitor* account continued,

> Zalmon H. Shapiro, the company's owner and president, contended that at one point most of the material unaccounted for was probably to be found in burial pits at the plant. After many meetings and discussions, Mr. Shapiro was forced to have the buried materials dug up, but the results showed clearly that not more than about 5% of the more than 100 pounds unaccounted for at that stage could be recovered. The documents showed tyat Mr. Shapiro had several commercial contracts with Israel. His company was a sales agent for the Government of Israel through its Ministry of Defense. An FBI report said Mr. Shapiro was part of a "highly organized effort on the part of Israel in the United States to obtain substantial technical and financial assistance."

In the early months of 1978 — which is to say, a whole year before *National Review* published Bernard L. Cohen's emphatic assurances about "stringent safeguards" against theft at our nuclear plants — discussion of the Apollo diversions became much more open.

Had Dr. Cohen read only the David Burnham *Times* articles of January 26, February 28, and March 2, 1978, he would have known

1. that the CIA had "concluded as early as 1974 — two years earlier than previously indicated — that Israel had already produced atomic weapons, partly with uranium it had obtained by clandestine means";
2. that Lee V. Gossick, Executive Director of the Nuclear Regulatory Commission, who had originally told a Congressional committee that there was no evidence of theft

at the Apollo plant, had subsequently retracted that statement; and

3. that a CIA document had been inadvertently released disclosing that the CIA had informed President Johnson in 1968 that Israel had nuclear bombs made largely with the use of clandestinely procured materials, whereupon President Johnson had instructed the agency "not to tell anyone else, not even Dean Rusk and Robert MacNamara."

Most interesting is Burnham's account of Lee V. Gossick's initial appearance before the House Subcommittee on Energy and Environment, which was looking into reports of thefts at nuclear plants. "At one point in his testimony," Burnham wrote, the Executive Director of the NRC "said that every possible case of diversion had been investigated, and we have no evidence that a significant amount of special nuclear material was stolen. A few minutes later, when specifically asked about Apollo, Mr. Gossick said he was not familiar with alleged circumstances about that." Two days later, Gossick in fact "acknowledged that his first statement was not 'in full compliance' with the obligation to keep Congress 'fully and currently informed.' " But by then the House subcommittee was hearing testimony from Dr. Victor Gilinsky, one of the four sitting commissioners of the nuclear agency, who acknowledged that, with respect to the Apollo facility, "the Commission's obligation to keep Congress informed had not been 'discharged in the manner I would want to do it in the future,' and that Mr. Gossick's original statement 'really does not pass muster.' "

The revelation about President Johnson's order to the CIA, through its director, Richard N. Helms, not to tell his Secretaries of State and Defense about the "Apollo-Israel diversions" was part of a four-page interview with Carl Duckett, the CIA's former deputy director for science and technology, inadvertently included in a 550-page report by the NRC concerning what the Commission knew or did not know about the possible theft of nuclear material that could be made into atomic bombs. Mr. Duckett had discussed the Apollo situation with the heads of the nuclear agency, and he recalls that, when details were being laid out, one commissioner had commented with mock jocularity: "My God, I almost went to work with Zal Shapiro. I came close to working for him." David Burnham then adds: "Dr. Edward A. Mason, who was a Commissioner in 1976 and who is now a Vice President of the Standard Oil Company . . . confirmed in a telephone conversation today (March 2, 1978) that he had made approximately the statement attributed to him and that he was referring to Dr. Zalmon Shapiro, the former President of a nuclear facility in Apollo, Pennsylvania."

On March 23, 1978, when there was no longer any possibility of further blanket concealment of nuclear theft — except perhaps from readers of Bernard L. Cohen's articles in *National Review* — the *Washington Star* published this summary:

> The AEC decided in 1966 to conceal a loss of nuclear materials from the public on the ground that premature disclosure "could lead to sensational and probably inaccurate press reports." According to a previously secret document made public today by the Senate Government Affairs Committee, the issue was the unexplained loss of 202 pounds of highly enriched uranium from a plant in Apollo, Pennsylvania. . . . Howard C. Brown, then the Agency's General Manger, conceded that because the safeguard system then rested on a "presumption of honesty" it "might not reveal a deliberate and systematic attempt to divert nuclear material to a foreign government." AEC officials resolved their problems by developing a "theory" that the company had lost the uranium by consistently underestimating its waste over a number of years.

Just to round out our account to this point, we should note that by March, 1978, Paul Leventhal had published his book about the "case of the phantom uranium ship" that had vanished for a few days back in 1968. Leventhal called his book *The Plumbat Affair,* because the "220 tons of uranium" that disappeared from the ship had been carried in drums mislabeled "Plumbat." In an Op-Ed article for the *Times* Leventhal observed that "belated detection of a diversion, as in the Plumbat case, offers no guarantee that the diversion will be publicly announced and acted upon"; and as for the gravity of that particular diversion, he added: "The use of this material in reactors of the type operating in Israel ... at the time could produce enough products of plutonium for as many as 40 atomic bombs over 20 years."

During the course of 1978 the revelations about nuclear diversions for purposes of smuggling, as also about real and staged hijackings for purposes of clandestine purchase of materials suitable for the manufacture of atomic bombs, were making the facts so well known that the bureaucrats who anticipated deeper and deeper Congressional or news media inquiries began making public moves to cover themselves. Even so, as of March 21, 1979, the cover-up on the Apollo situation was still very much in effect. On that date David Burnham revealed in the *Times* that the General Accounting Office had accused the Attorney General and the Director of the CIA of illegally blocking the access of Congressional investigators to secret intelligence files.

We should perhaps mention here, for purposes of background, that under a purposely broad grant of authority from Congress the GAO is legally entitled to have easy access to classified documents in the executive branch. All agencies are required to furnish any information and documents that GAO's investigators request — the only exemption, under the law, as Burnham noted, being information as to "specific funds requested by either the head of the CIA or the Attorney General for an unforeseen emergency."

Specifically, what prompted Burnham's comments on the subject in late March, 1979, was disclosure of the contents of a letter from the Comptroller General of the United States, Elmer B. Staats, to the chairman of the House Subcommittee on Energy and Power — Democratic Representative Dingell of Michigan — in which the Comptroller General charged that, in 1978, the GAO was refused permission to examine classified data about the uranium discovered missing from the Apollo plant fifteen years ago. When asked about the Comptroller General's charge, spokesmen for both the CIA and the Attorney General, Burnham noted, refused to comment. Mr. Staats had written to Representative Dingell, Burnham further noted, because Dingell had charged in a letter of December 27, 1978, that failure to allow a full Congressional investigation of the uranium unaccounted for at the Apollo plant "raised basic questions about the performance of the FBI, the CIA, and other agencies in attempting to determine whether the material was stolen."

There is a piece of powerful irony here. The evidence is abundant that the FBI and CIA had done their duty and that high elective and appointive officials had engaged in a cover-up. Yet, when Representative Dingell's charges were first disclosed, John Shattuck and Jerry J. Berman of the American Civil Liberties Union (ACLU), David Cohen of Common Cause, and Morton H. Halperin of the Center for National Security Studies used the disclosure rather cynically to attack the FBI and the CIA as being "still out of control."

The reality, we must not hesitate to say, is that Presidents Johnson, Nixon, Ford, and now Carter have connived in the Apollo diversions cover-up. And with this particular cover-up the media have been unusually compliant. In fact, the media and top-level political figures have cunningly contrived through various sleights-of-hand to obvert the entire situation. For what are at best partisan electoral concerns and at worst interests of conspiratorial collusion with operatives of foreign nations, responsibility has been shifted away from the high officials in ultimate control of the security agencies to the agencies themselves.

In a syndicated column released for publication on November 16, 1977, Garry Wills, who used to be an editor and major contributor of *National Review,* had observed that the "story of Israel's hijackings and smugglings of enriched uranium raises troubling questions." Having seen the evidence then available about German phantom freighters and uranium diversions in Pennsylvania, Wills charged the American Government with what he said amounted to complicity in potential nuclear blackmail. "Our Government," he charged, was certainly "as complicitous as Germany's in creating another nuclear power. The commandos did not have to seize our uranium, because we were quietly slipping it to them."

But why not slip uranium for atomic bombs to Israel? Don't we, doesn't the entire West "owe it" to the Israelis — "as survivors of the holocaust" — to provide them with ultimate weapons of resistance in the Mideast? Garry Wills's answer, addressed to a readership made up primarily of readers highly sympathetic to the national security needs of Israel, ran as follows:

> Israel is currently our ally. But George Washington warned, in his Farewell Address, against presuming the nation will forever maintain the same relations of friendship and hostility. A different sort of regime, or an Israeli panic into irresponsible action, might possess a blackmail power over us if we help give them the bomb. The country can make demands of this sort: "Give us all the non-nuclear weapons we want, to use any way we want, or we will be forced to use the nuclear bomb you helped us get." Are we willing to

support any Israeli action under that kind of blackmail? These questions become more acute when we remember that Israeli Prime Minister Menachem Begin may have his finger on the nuclear button. A man with heart trouble, recently hospitalized for exhaustion, with a terrorist background and maximal demands on territory — are we sure we would support any action he might take against the inhabitants of the West Bank?

Those are fair questions — given the fact that the United States has never shown a comparable concern to "slip" materials for weapons of ultimate security to other "embattled allies" in Southeast Asia, Africa, or South America, for instance. And perhaps, had he still been on good terms with his old friends at *National Review,* Mr. Wills might conceivably have been called upon to raise questions of that kind for the "Prometheus Bound" issue of February, 1979, to counterbalance some of Dr. Cohen's exaggerations in the opposite direction.

Dr. Cohen's arguments for breeder reactors and against worrying about safeguards at nuclear plants, as well as those of B. Bruce-Briggs that we briefly touched on, qualify as conservative or "right wing" arguments only because they were published in *National Review* and purportedly take the side of "free enterprise" — at Apollo, Pennsylvania, and elsewhere — against the "antinuclear lobbyists" of the left. But in substance they are arguments, we need to stress, that simply repeat the analysis of the uses of terrorism supplied by Lenin in *Partisan Warfare* and Trotsky in various works. Both of them had contended, long before they actually organized the terror of their Russian Revolution, that neither terrorism nor guerrilla warfare was sufficient to overthrow the capitalist state. As capitalism developed, they both reasoned, state power grew stronger and more concentrated. Terrorist instruments, therefore, could be at best only adjuncts to the mass convulsive uprising.

But in this Trotsky and Lenin were both wrong. They failed to take account — as Georges Sorel later explained in *Reflections on Violence* — of the unwillingness of bourgeois-liberal elites to use the power at their command. They also failed to realize the significance of the enormous developments occurring in the technology of weapons.

It is absurd at this late date to go on pretending that, because no commando units or hit teams of powerful revolutionary organizations or "potential adversaries" have actually seized a nuclear plant for terrorist purposes, the thing is unlikely or even impossible. If it starts to happen, it need not happen often to produce its most devastating effects. Those able to do such a thing will obviously not do it before they are prepared to carry through some overall design for our government collapse. In March, 1979, *U.S. News and World Report* published an article, prepared with the full cooperation of Federal agencies, concerning what officials look upon as the "inevitability of terrorist attempts to go after nuclear bombs." In brief: "To these officials, it isn't a question of whether such an attack will be made but where and when."

Yet far more ominous was the article's acknowledgment that all current safeguard measures are based on the assumption that the attacking bands of terrorists would consist of fifteen members or less. All the safeguards currently ordered (though by no means effectively implemented) become irrelevant, one highly competent official said, if you assume that the goal of terrorists is not to blow up a city but to use the nuclear weapon for high-stakes political blackmail.

The *U.S. News and World Report* article appeared shortly before the Three Mile Island news story broke on April 4, 1979. And in a sense that story served, with its environmental domestic emphasis, to distract attention from the graver nuclear safeguard problems. Already the

Three Mile Island story has passed into a pure entertainment phase. The plant has become a tourist attraction. People come for picnic lunches in the vicinity, with picnic tables and other facilities, including an instructive film, provided by the power company. The impression is emerging that the "near catastrophe" has proved to be highly instructive, that it marks a turning point for the better, and perhaps even for the very best, in nuclear age safeguards. But let us now review a bit of the transcript of conversations at the meetings of the NRC that took place during the course of the crisis. Certainly they reveal much about the attitudes and competence of the men charged with advising our President on our nuclear security needs. According to the account in the *Times,* we learn from the transcript that, at the very moment President Carter was on his way to tour the plant, the NRC's

technical experts believed that there was enough oxygen gas in a hydrogen bubble over the reactor core to cause a fire in the reactor vessel . . . . The commissioners were still feverishly working on the wording of documents concerning possible evacuations as Mr. Carter toured the plant. . . . They [the transcripts] indicate that the five commissioners and the agency's technical staff were, at times, near despair because of sketchy information about the reactor and difficulty of evaluating unforeseen events. .. . Dr. Hendrie said at one point, "When I say 6 to 12 hours once things begin to go, and you figure it's going to go, you know that there's nothing else you can press or pull in the way of switches and [are] going to have to let it run its course and the best thing to do is to just get away. This could take several hours — four hours, three-four hours, at least, to work its way through the vessel."
Commissioner . . . Kennedy then asked if that was from the "beginning of the event."
Dr. Hendrie replied: "Well, that's from the point where you say, 'Oh boy, you know, it's gone, we've lost it.' ". . . [Mr. Mattson said:] "I'm not sure why we're not moving people.

Got to say it, I have been saying it down here: I don't know what we are protecting at this point, I think we ought to be moving people." . . .

Discussing the President's trip to the plant, Jack Warner, the spokesman for the Secret Service, said today that the agency responsible for protecting the President had not been told that any NRC personnel believed the hydrogen bubble was near the point of flammability. . . .

The transcripts also revealed that Harold R. Denton, the director of reactor regulation who was the President's representative and took over accident control operations and press briefings, arrived at the plant March 30 and recommended a limited evacuation. . . . However, in his several telephone conversations with Governor Thornburgh, Dr. Hendrie did not recommend a general evacuation, only that people stay indoors and that pregnant women and pre-school children move away from the plant area. . . .

There was great preoccupation with the wording — and at one point even the spelling of the word imminent — in press statements and policy statements.

Dr. Hendrie was told that "Mr. Rafshoon's office wants somebody for the McNeil-Lehrer show tonight," . . . And Dr. Hendrie, at one time, asked: "Which amendment is it that guarantees freedom of the press? Well, I'm against it." . . .

Commissioner Bradford at one point on Sunday asked Robert Budnitz, deputy director of regulatory research, if he was "pretty confident" about one factor in a calculation about the bubble.

"No," replied Mr. Budnitz, who later remarked: "One thing I have found out, this agency needs a chemist." . . .

At one point [Dr. Hendrie] also said that, as a result of the accident, "We'll probably enter — what is it? — probably four to five months of over-regulation of the nuclear industry."

Commissioner Kennedy asked, "As contrasted with what?"

Although the media dutifully traced violations at this particular plant back to 1978 (as of May, 1979), had they been more industrious they would have discovered certain other problems that had occurred somewhat earlier. As a result of documents released through a Freedom of Information Act suit by Ralph Nader's Congress Watch, it was revealed in March, 1976 (almost three years to the day before the Three Mile Island crisis) that the NRC had proposed fining Metropolitan Edison's Three Mile Island plant $8,000 (coffee money for a corporation) after the company's security force failed to apprehend "a disturbed former employee who entered the protected area around the utility's nuclear reactor." The NRC said that an electrician who had been working on a construction project there drove his car onto the island, scaled a fence eight feet high, moved around the security area for about an hour, and finally left before being apprehended. The NRC said that the company was being fined not only for failure to block the entry of the "disturbed" man and to apprehend him, but also because neither the company management nor the state police was immediately informed of the intrusion as mandated by the security plan. A spokesman for the company said it had decided no useful purpose would be served by prosecuting the former employee.

The NRC documents also revealed that this same plant had been the subject of three bomb threats — September 23, 1972, March 23, 1973, and November 5, 1973. And it revealed too that the proposed $8,000 fine was the second time that Metropolitan Edison had been cited for poor security. On November 26, 1974, the AEC fined it $3,500 after a Government inspector successfully entered the plant without being stopped.

The response to the Three Mile Island crisis from such enthusiastic proponents of nuclear power as *National Review,* Dr. Cohen, and Mr. Buckley has been a deafening silence.

PART II

Terrorism's "Infinite Variety"

1. Chemical, Biological, and Other Instruments of Mass Destruction

IN JUNE, 1976, several large corporations reported receiving letter bombs after having ignored earlier extortion letters demanding they place payments in bank accounts in Matamoros, Mexico. According to one company official, the FBI found that extortion demands had been sent the previous fall to two hundred business executives in large companies. One letter stated: "The secret is that B. A. Fox (the extortionist) has a fine bacteria lab, well-stocked with various types of bacteria, viruses, germs — ranging from simple staph type infections up to and including rabies."

In an unrelated story the same day the Associated Press quoted a declassified CIA study on terrorism:

We should expect to witness steadily greater and more wide-spread sophistication in targeting, execution and weaponry. And while most groups will probably continue to be deterred by both moral considerations and calculations of the risk involved, the danger that a fanatic few might resort to weapons of mass destruction will increase accordingly. Such weapons might include nuclear bombs, but more likely would involve chemical, biological and radiological agents. In contrast to nuclear devices, many of these are presently relatively easy to acquire. Hence the danger that they could turn up in the hands of the sort of ultraradical or psychopathic fringe group that would have the fewest compunctions about using them is very real. Whether or not weapons of mass destruction are actually brought into play, the odds are that the impact of terror will be more sharply felt in the United States in the years just ahead.

One basic conclusion of the study was that this country should follow a more flexible policy in dealing with terrorist situations, as contrasted with the rigid "no concessions" policy currently in effect. But as we noted earlier, that policy was no longer in effect.

Chemical and biological agents are easier both to manufacture on one's own and to hijack. If plutonium is hardly guarded at all, chemical and biological agents are guarded even less. For example, in describing an 840-acre island involved in virological research the *Times* (February 23, 1975) wrote: "There are enough viruses on this small, lovely island to destroy all the livestock in the world. The shores of the island are guarded by a small force of guards armed with small arms. There are armed guards that control the beaches and keep away intruders, particularly vacationers in the summer months who sometimes drift here in sailboats." The article noted also that there had been numerous efforts to get the Federal Government to open up at least a part of the island to the general public for recreation purposes! But if vacationers can drift in casually and dawdle on the beach a few hours before being noticed, what a terrorist group might do is quite evident. It could easily hold hostage a nation or a city, as experts such as Brian Jenkins of the Rand Corporation predict will be a common occurrence during the next decade.

The National Advisory Committee report (March 2, 1977), referred to earlier, emphatically warned that the danger from high technology weapons to Americans is so great that unusually tough measures may be needed to protect the public. The main conclusion of the panel of Government experts was that the threat of attack by terrorists armed with nuclear, biological, or chemical weapons "is very real and ought to be realistically and urgently faced." The panel concluded, however, that the danger of casualties from biological weapons is even greater than that from nuclear or chemical ones. One example, described in detail in the study, is the use of either bacteria or fungi that cause anthrax or cryptococcosis infections.

> An attacker might simply drive through a medium-sized city using a truck-mounted dispenser. During spring or summer, this type of apparatus would not raise questions in most locales. Anyone exposed for two minutes would probably inhale enough to be infected. Not all the victims would receive lethal doses, but the medical-care problems associated with tens of thousands of cases of anthrax infection in themselves would be catastrophic for a community.

Another threat scenario involves the release of as little as a single ounce of either the anthrax or cryptococcosis agent into the air-circulation system of a domed stadium. Within an hour 70,000 persons would be infected.

R. W. Mengel of the BDM Corporation, who prepared the section of the report on sophisticated, high-technology weapons, stressed that the U.S. is especially vulnerable to such attacks because it is so technologically developed and its people so mobile. He concluded that the only reason it has not yet happened is that no terrorist group has been able to "combine the necessary physical resources with technicians who are motivated to engage in an activity that could potentially kill thousands of people." That offers scant hope for the future. Indeed, Mengel appears to overestimate the level of technical expertise and physical resources necessary to fabricate such megadeath weapons. Many are easy to make or widely available for purchase or theft. How easy is evident from a *Time* report of February 11, 1977, that a British military laboratory (the Microbiological Research Establishment) was quite openly promoting the sale by mail of infectious bacteriological organisms. The otherwise secrecy-shrouded laboratory had begun the sale several years before, the Defense Ministry admitted, and in December, 1976, it had taken large display advertisements in a widely circulated science magazine, *Nature*. "Bacteria by the kilogram," the ads proclaimed in half-inch-high letters. "For listed items, please send your official order and delivery instructions. We can now supply these and more than 50 other products, including bacterial cell pastes, bacteriophages, animal viruses, and purified microbial products, especially enzymes and toxic proteins to any destination."

Because the sales were now being promoted so openly, they came to the attention of several members of the House of Commons and scientists, who expressed fears that terrorist customers could easily purchase them and contaminate entire cities. The justification offered for the sales was to defray some of the laboratory's costs. The Defense Ministry assured the House of Commons that these little "goodies" are supplied "only to bona fide customers at recognized laboratories or research institutes and dispatched in full conformity with international regulations for transmission of materials of this type by post or air." Since they were conducting a mail-order business, that claim seems a bit inflated. Moreover, as Dr. George H. Connell of the Center for Disease Control in Atlanta explained (in connection with another matter), "There is no such thing as a microorganism that can't cause trouble." And Dr. Matthew Meselson, chairman of Harvard's Biochemistry and Molecular Biology Department, has pointed out that many organisms (such as anthrax), though fairly common in soil, don't usually cause infection. But if they are dispersed in an aerosol spray, they can, because the tiny particles can then reach the lungs.

It was noted by critics, however, that there was no suggestion the orders being filled by the British military laboratory were subject to Government scrutiny. Among the products listed were three strains of *Escherichia coli*. According to James Reynolds of the London Pharmaceutical Society, a terrorist with no particular expertise could feed the bacteria into the water system or other public facilities. The cost? Two of the coli strains are offered in minimum lots of one kilogram for $111, and the third strain in 100-gram quantities for $171. (Such prices would no doubt be of major aid in defraying the expenses of the laboratory.) Although, Reynolds said, the organisms were not unusually virulent, "a kilo of organisms is quite a fantastic amount." And while one kilogram "might not" harm a city the size of London, several kilograms would be enough to defeat the antibacterial agents in the water system. The advertisement was also offering 100-gram quantities of *Haemophilus influenzae* at $255. Some strains of this organism have been associated with lung infections, notably bronchitis and pneumonia. The Ministry noted in passing that over the last year it had sold bacteria to customers in nine West European countries.

Another leading candidate for terrorist use is highly lethal VX nerve gas. U.S. Government sources have admitted that some of their stocks of this agent are currently missing and unaccounted for. There have been known instances of its being rather casually offered for sale in New York City. The Army announced in April, 1977, that it planned to dispose of several batches of obsolete chemical warfare agents, some of them lethal. The batches, ranging in size from less than an ounce to as much as 100.4 ounces, were in glass bottles, pellets, and other forms. They are stored in ten different states. And if some of these facilities may have been adequately guarded, others were not. Two of the facilities, which the Army conveniently listed and the media made public, were the Brooklyn Army Base and the Freeport Naval Reserve Center on Long Island. And those facilities have less security than a local supermarket.

But it is not necessary to go to even that minimal degree of bother to obtain VX nerve gas. Both the U.S. and Great Britain have declassified and widely published the formula for making it. It could be produced by any competent scientist or graduate student with access to a good laboratory. And merely making it and having it in one's possession would not in itself be a crime. According to Dr. Meselson of Harvard, we have no law prohibiting a person from developing, producing, or stockpiling biological or chemical warfare agents. Treaties "prohibit" nations from doing certain things with them, but not individuals. What might a terrorist do with VX? A canister dropped from any tall building or sprayed over a large city from a private plane would kill millions.

Other agents are still easier to fabricate. In 1968 there was the much-publicized Weathermen-Yippy threat (attempt?) to "space-out" the delegates to the Democratic National Convention in Chicago, and everyone else in Chicago as well, by dumping LSD into Lake Michigan, the city's water source. According to Chicago officials, the water filtration system would have defeated (perhaps did?) the LSD. But in 1972, in Chicago the neo-Nazi "Order of the Rising Sun" was apprehended with some 80 pounds of typhoid bacillus they had themselves manufactured. They had intentions, it seems, of dropping it into the water systems of Chicago, St. Louis, and other Middle Western cities. This time Chicago officials were far less confident that the filtration chemicals would have defeated the typhoid. It is known that the Army, for example, has developed virus strains that survive filtration chemicals, as well as spore-hardened anthrax that would live, kill, and go on doing so for some twenty years. The people in possession of the typhoid bacillus, it should be emphasized, were not picked up as a result of intelligence activity; they were caught only by a fluke, when their car was stopped for another reason. The police, apparently engaging in one of those practices professional civil libertarians find so distasteful and crypto-fascist, happened to discover the typhoid bacillus in a search of the car. R. W. Mengel of the BDM Corporation seems to have been wrong, then, when he explained the lack of any *major* terrorist action of this nature as due to a failure thus far to combine the necessary physical resources with radically motivated technicians. It seems rather to be due to benevolent chance or Divine Providence that it has not yet happened.

Advisedly, we stated that no major incident — apparently — has yet occurred. But a number of actual, probable, or possible ones have occurred. The *Seattle Times* revealed on November 20, 1970, that an informant had "notified the U.S. Customs Bureau that the revolutionary Weatherman Organization is planning to steal biological weapons from Ft. Detrick, Md., and contaminate a major city's water supply, the Army said yesterday. . . . The informant reported that the Weatherman members plan to obtain the biological materials by blackmailing a homosexual lieutenant at Ft. Detrick, the Army said, confirming an account in Jack Anderson's syndicated column. . . . The plan's aim is to cause havoc, he said, and increase possibilities of revolution."

On November 7, 1976, the *Boston Globe* reported that Libya had become the center for international terrorism, in particular nerve gas terrorism. It told of the concern of two European nations and of a little-publicized incident that had occurred about six months earlier in the United States when nerve gas had been seized by security people.

On February 24, 1977, the New York *Daily News* described a nerve gas threat that "nearly caused" a crisis in the city in 1972. The threat, not made public at the time, was to contaminate the water system, and it brought city officials to the verge of declaring a "health emergency." It caused a frantic week of committee meetings and strategy conferences. According to the *Daily News*, "city officials ultimately concluded that the threat had not been carried out and details of the episode were filed away from public view." As usual, the officials were right on top of things, waiting and hoping that something unpleasant would eventually go away. According to the two *News* reporters, city water officials refused to discuss the seven-day drama for fear it would plant ideas in the minds of potential terrorists. However, other health, police, military, and security officials involved in the crisis were willing to discuss it, because, they believed, the story would reassure the citizens that the city was fully prepared to handle such a man-made disaster. Police Commissioner Codd assured everyone that his department has contingency plans "for all kinds of disasters," but cautioned that the details are kept secret. From whom, one wonders, in the light of multimillion-dollar heroin robberies from the Police Department itself? However, a spokesman for the Mayor's Emergency Control Board, which coordinates the various agencies when a disaster occurs, was constrained to concede that the Board does not have any master plan for coordination in the event of such a disaster.

The threat, contained in a letter from Australia to a radio station in Detroit, was to dump nerve gas into the city's Kensico Reservoir in Westchester. It was taken seriously by the FBI, which alerted city officials. One emergency director was quoted as saying that scientists had told them that "anyone with resources and determination could poison our water system." The only recourse then was to prepare hospitals to receive the victims, police agencies to deal with the panic and chaos, and the Municipal Broadcasting System to make emergency announcements. The city was incapable of any response beyond that!

"On the first frantic day," the then City Health Commissioner said, "we realized we knew next to nothing about the gas and we had no way to even test for its presence in our water system." Experts from the United Nations (of all places), colleges, and finally one from Edgewood Army Arsenal were brought in. The Army expert alleviated their fears by advising that it would take tons of nerve gas to poison the 31-billion-gallon reservoir. He also established a testing system and other emergency procedures that have since become standard for such cases. It was, then, merely the terrorist's method of delivery that was at fault, if the Army expert was right. Had the terrorist threatened to drop only a bucketful of nerve gas off the World Trade Center, it would have been effective both as a threat and if carried out.

Still, there are many chemicals that can, quite easily, make an area's water system lethal. On June 5, 1977, a North Carolina reservoir was effectively sabotaged. Although the *Times* made no mention of it, the wire services reported on the action. Safety caps and valves were removed, and poison chemicals were sent into the reservoir.

The perpetrators, a company official commented, certainly knew exactly what they were doing. The purpose was not revealed. Water had to be brought in.

Within days of the revelation of the nerve gas threat to New York City two other rather suspicious and unexplained incidents occurred. On February 20 the AP reported that a cloud of poisonous chlorine gas had "leaked out" of a Dow Chemical plant in Louisiana, but dissipated before causing serious injuries or requiring evacuations. Although a Dow spokesman said a tank had ruptured, initial reports by the State Police and sheriff's deputies said there had been an explosion. The plant was only twenty miles south of Baton Rouge, where on December 10, 1976, about 10,000 persons were evacuated when a 42-mile-long cloud of chlorine had "leaked out" of an Allied Chemical plant (which, incidentally, has one of the worst records for such accidents, if that is what they are).

Also on February 20 the *Times* reported a carbon tetrachloride "spill" down the Ohio River: "Who spilled 70 tons of carbon tetrachloride into the Ohio River system, forcing the inhabitants to boil their drinking water two days ago to rid it of the potentially dangerous chemical?" Although the Environmental Protection Agency had been investigating the matter since February 6, it was not thought fit to inform the public until twelve days later. Of the four companies in the area from which the "spill" could have originated, one (an FMC Corporation plant) was regarded as the most suspect, since, unlike the other plants, it refused to allow its discharges to be sampled and inspected. What is most amazing, however, is that a corporation can successfully and legitimately refuse to allow the EPA to inspect its discharges when an entire river system serving as a public water supply is being poisoned with a deadly chemical. Also significant is that the entire massive spill had "slipped by" the filtration system in Cincinnati. According to the EPA's regional administrator, "What we were looking for was the possibility that somebody may have increased normal discharges. We never expected to find numbers indicative of a spill, and that's what we found." He confirmed that there was probably more than one spill.

Whether such incidents (of which there are scores each year) are terrorist actions, not-so-dry-run testings, accidents, or the result of negligence is irrelevant. What matters is that they are pathetically easy to effectuate if a prospective terrorist so desires.

Just how easy it all is was made abundantly clear by another incident, reported by the UPI on March 20, 1977: "Most of the people in Iowa could have been killed or crippled by highly toxic PCB that was mistakenly trucked into the state as oil to be spread on gravel roads, an official of the State Department of Environmental Quality says." Luckily, the shipment was identified before it had been spread over the roads. Apparently, a waste-oil dealer in Minnesota, who owed money to a company in Omaha, offered to pay his bill with waste oil from a storage site in St. Paul. The Omaha drivers, in loading the oil, also took ink sludge and solvent contaminated with PCB. Again, the point is that such incidents can be done easily by a purposeful terrorist in our highly technological, mobile, industrialized society. It requires merely changing a label or two.

One of the most widely publicized and suspicious incidents was "legionnaires' disease." There was some speculation that it was an effectiveness test by terrorists. *U.S. News & World Report* disclosed (September 13, 1976) that "one facet of the widening investigation of the killer disease that struck American Legionnaires at their recent Philadelphia Convention has been kept largely undercover. The fact is that the FBI has been, and still is, in the thick of the search for the cause of the mysterious ailment — indicating sabotage has not been ruled out." And Jack

Anderson wrote in his column that Congressional investigators believed that "a demented veteran or paranoid
anti-military type" with a rudimentary knowledge of
chemistry may have been responsible. Quoting from a
"Secret Classified" study, Anderson rather recklessly
provided the exact details as to how it could be done, and
done quite simply. He cited a statement by Dr. William
Sunderman, Jr., described by the investigators as the
nation's leading expert on nickel poisoning, which offered
this startling conclusion: "The exposure to nickel carbonyl
must have been introduced willfully, because the quantity
found in the tissue of the victims could not otherwise be
explained." His conclusion, according to Anderson, was
supported by (again quoting the secret study) "an
anonymous, ominous-sounding letter," mailed before the
incident had attracted national attention, which "referred
to substances containing nickel carbonyl and discussed
the murder and killing of authority and military-type
figures."

Several sources have also reported that during the
Six-Day Arab-Israeli War (1967), when Israeli forces
overran Egyptian bunkers, they found two large lots of
nerve gas supplied by the USSR. Pictures of the caches
were provided by the Israelis. Even earlier, when Saudi
Arabia and Nasser's Egypt were fighting a war by proxy
in South Yemen during the 1960's, it was established that
Egyptian forces actually used various types of poison
gases provided by the USSR. However, the significance of
both incidents from the standpoint of terrorism, in the
judgment of intelligence experts, is that the USSR was
clearly willing to have the chemical warfare agents fall
into the hands of Palestinian extremists, since they could
readily obtain them in various ways from the Egyptian
forces.

KGB involvement in the dispersal of these agents is
extensive. According to declassified CIA reports, the

USSR has recently opened an enormous new research center to develop bacteriological weapons. Such developments mean that the probabilities for terrorist acquisition of these weapons are increasing rapidly. The USSR is also reportedly training a minimum of 1,200 terrorists annually at an institute in Moscow, and many of these, it has been established, are now in the U.S.

In another actual incident in late 1976 traffic came to a sudden halt on one of the two major bridges in San Francisco as drivers stopped their cars, rubbing their eyes. Small quantities of tear gas, stolen from a National Guard armory, had been released on the bridge by pranksters — or perhaps terrorists conducting a test. Suppose it had been a lethal agent. In fact, at about the same time, the counterterrorist unit of the San Francisco Police Department reported it had apprehended a terrorist with homemade nerve gas.

Moving from actual and suspicious incidents to possibilities, one interesting chemical option for terrorists is fluorocarbons. On May 11, 1977, three Federal agencies urged that, since such gases deplete the earth's ozone layer, they should be phased out and banned within two years. FDA Commissioner Donald Kennedy pointed out that they thereby subject all of us to an increased risk of skin cancer and an increased risk of environmental change causing altered climates and adverse crop conditions.

Already in 1974 Lowell Ponte (a self-described former expert in bizarre weapons for the Pentagon) suggested in his widely discussed *The Cooling* that we consider the frightening scenario in which terrorists acting in conjunction with a radicalized Third World nation attach fluorocarbon gases and bromine canisters to weather balloons that release their gases twenty miles above the ground. The industrialized Caucasian nations would, Ponte said, have no alternative but to yield to their demands. He quoted Harvard University Atmospheric Sciences Professor Michael B. McElroy as having written in June, 1975, that the injection of bromine gas into the upper atmosphere by airplane, small rocket, or balloon could punch a hole in the ozone layer that would remain stationary above a given latitude while the earth turned under it. Remaining open for days or weeks, it would expose everyone under it to dangerous doses of ultraviolet radiation. In McElroy's view, "it would be a doomsday weapon because it would cause equal harm to friend and foe alike." But according to Ponte, "in this last judgment McElroy is wrong, for the increases in ultraviolet radiation that a thinning of the ozone layer would cause can directly do far more damage to Caucasians than to people with protective skin pigmentation. Thus, an attack on the ozone layer can be a race-specific weapon of war, and might seem an ideal tool to a racist fanatic — an apt answer to triage policies he sees as genocidal. (Food triage is selling or giving whatever food is available to those nations with the best chance of survival, rather than spreading it so thin that it doesn't help anyone.) In this Ponte is mistaken. The effect would be as much on climate and crops as upon human beings and would thus affect those other than Caucasians, if in a different way.

What characterizes the best-selling works on terrorism today, as pointed out in the Introduction, is the lack of any adequate discussion of the possible uses of technological instruments of megadeath destruction. Two notable exceptions to this trend are Brian Jenkins (*High Technology Terrorism*) and Lowell Ponte in several articles in various journals. Ponte was with the Pentagon as a deputy to Theodore B. Taylor and later, as he himself describes it, "a specialist in terrorist, bizarre, and environmental weapons with International Research and Technology Corporation, a Pentagon-consulted think tank in

Washington." Since he is evidently plugged into the right sources, and is utilizing that information, it is worth dwelling on at length, and critically examining, some of his comments and analyses, in particular those contained in an article in *Gallery* (May, 1977), "The Terrorists' War on American Cities," an extract from his book, *The Terrorizing.*

Ponte justified the publication of such interesting megadeath scenarios by insisting that he is "not telling sophisticated terrorists anything they don't already know." Perhaps that is so, though we doubt it. The key word is "sophisticated." He is most certainly telling quite a lot of not-so-sophisticated terrorists, potential terrorists, and unstable persons how to paralyze major American metropolitan areas and even cause the deaths of hundreds of thousands, if not millions, of innocent persons. It is one thing to discuss such techniques in think tanks or professional journals; it is quite another to discuss them in mass circulation "girlie" magazines like *Gallery*, or in a book he obviously hopes will become a best seller. He is, in short, geometrically escalating the whole problem. More appropriately, however, at the outset of his article he expresses the hope that the reader will have nightmares after reading it, and that unless he gets upset enough to demand that his public officials take adequate safeguards against terrorism, he may confidently expect that some of these threat scenarios will occur.

As is the custom with well-connected writers, Ponte went on the talk-show circuit to "hype" his article and book. One appearance was on the Arlene Francis Show on New York's WOR radio (April 13, 1977). During the interview Ms. Francis several times became so upset that it seemed she might not be able to carry on. She too, however, tartly queried whether he might not be providing prospective terrorists with rather horrifying instruments and fruitful suggestions. Again his reply was that any self-respecting terrorist knew all about these things. By way of additional justification, he compared himself analogously with Taylor when he went public with his warnings about nuclear theft and terrorism. Before then, Ponte said, when Taylor was still working within the Pentagon and sending confidential memos here and there, those responsible for nuclear security within the Pentagon contemptuously dismissed such warnings as far-fetched and not worth bothering about. And that, of course, is quite true, as we have noted earlier in regard to the comments by the then Secretary of Defense, James R. Schlesinger. But Ponte went on to make the incredibly ignorant, or merely self-serving, claim — as opposed to what Taylor himself had been saying — that since Taylor went public adequate safeguards against nuclear theft and terrorism had been provided! His hope then, he said, was that his writings would cause adequate safeguards to be provided against the weapons he was discussing.

We must, however, credit Ponte for his emphatic forewarning that "the threat is real and awesome." Like other experts he cautions that the technologies upon which we depend are highly centralized and, equally important, that the psychological makeup of most Americans is, from the terrorist standpoint, ideally fragile and easily fragmented by massive disruptions of that technology. The possibility of such large-scale economic and social disruptions, he states, gives Pentagon planners nightmares.

Ponte discusses threat scenarios from within the context of specific American cities. On the basis of the commonly-cited principle that an area's vulnerability is, in general, proportional to its centralization, Manhattan is the most dangerous place on earth, where everyone is, so to speak, living at ground-zero. He uses much space to dramatize, and probably overemphasize, various experiments conducted by the Army within the U.S. and originally made public by the Long Island paper *Newsday*. In 1966 light bulbs containing nonlethal bacteria were dropped at various points in the New York City subway system, which at that time was ridden by an estimated 4.4 million persons daily, about half the city's population. Of as much significance is the fact that a rather large percentage of these people then journeyed to the nearby bedroom suburbs. The result, according to a Pentagon-commissioned study by New York Survival Studies, is that it would be an excellent instrument. Millions would already have been exposed before one person fell ill with discernible symptoms. Immunization would be too late to help at that point. If hundreds of thousands of persons were severely incapacitated simultaneously, it would overwhelm the medical facilities. Effective treatment and isolation of so many people with a highly contagious disease would be impossible.

But there are additional factors not mentioned by Ponte in his recital of the details of this study. The ranks of the medical personnel themselves would have been decimated through the initial dispersal of the agent. Ponte might have noted too that immunization on such a massive scale, for those in surrounding areas not yet exposed, would be out of the question. No stockpiles of the large batches of immunizing agents are maintained. The drug companies needed more than half a year to develop the swine flu stocks. Most important, a secondary and perhaps more devastating effect (as in nuclear threat scenarios) would be the massive pandemic panic as millions tried to flee, and fought like animals in the streets when all major services ground to a halt because of a lack of key personnel. It would be, in short, an induced and completely effective general strike, that old Sorelian instrument of revolution that has for so long enthralled revolutionaries, although they have never been able to effectuate one through their revolutionary sermons to the masses.

On March 15, 1977, the Army said it had tested the White House ventilation system in 1962 to determine whether it was vulnerable to biological or chemical attack. In a brief statement, reported by the AP, the Army said that "at the request of the White House Staff [Kennedy's]" it had "tested the air-intake system of a portion of the White House." Army officials refused to divulge what substances were used or what conclusions were reached. They said the Carter White House staff would not let them say anything more. The statement was made in response to allegations made the previous week that the Army had conducted simulated biological warfare attacks on the White House, the Capitol (which the Army denied), and one Federal office building.

But, according to Ponte, the Army conducted mock biological warfare tests in 1950 that "contaminated" the Pentagon and several key Government buildings through air-conditioning and water systems. That much, he says, the Army now admits. Then, in the finest tradition of American journalism's literature of exposure and government-by-leaks, Ponte (drawing on information acquired through his past Government and Government-related employment), spices up his article with additional accounts, which he says have not yet been admitted by the Army. In 1970-71, he maintains, an assault group from Fort Detrick carried out a successful penetration of the White House and the Capitol buildings with mock chemical agents. Their conclusion was that if something like VX had been used, the President and most of Congress would have been killed. Merely breaking a vial of a lethal agent in the tourist areas of the White House would have been sufficient because of the conveniently centralized air-conditioning. The Fort Detrick group acted, Ponte says, without the knowledge of the Secret Service, the FBI, or Capitol Hill Police Department. He claims they also conducted a successful mock assassination of Kennedy in 1961.

Another fascinating opportunity for terrorists brought to our (and their) attention by Ponte concerns the storage sites for chemical and bacteriological weapons at Denver and Salt Lake City, and at the other sites that the media is always dutifully listing for us. Although they are well guarded, if an airliner should go down on one of these sites (there have already been several near misses), the result could be catastrophic. Many terrorist groups already have an abundance of Soviet SAM rockets. They are fairly cheap, light in weight, and can be operated even by a child, as well as being most effective. There have, of course, been several narrow escapes when terrorists were apprehended as they were about to use SAMs. There have been other incidents of plane "crashes" with scores of deaths in which it was concluded that a SAM rocket had been used. Ponte provides a great many other enticing scenarios, but we think our sampling is adequate to illustrate the point.

Despite his disclaimers, merely reading Ponte's article can give anyone more than enough information to make a very credible threat. What then? The Government would probably not cave in and accede to the demands. But that can mean only that it has to happen first before anything is done. If the Government does give in, then that means that the mere credible threat is enough. Both alternatives are frightening.

One point that Ponte stresses correctly, along with many other specialists, is the important interconnection between climatological changes (which will significantly affect food production), the depletion of energy resources, and technological terrorism.

The recent two-year drought in California brings into focus those interconnections among food production, energy, nuclear power, water supply systems, and the manifold opportunities for terrorists to disrupt the whole interrelated system by interdicting one part of it. The worst drought in modern California history lasted for twelve years (1892-1904). The question now is how long the next one will last. The coastal plain of southern California — where half the state's population lives — is basically so arid that for the past fifty years it has depended on imported water, which may come from as far away as Wyoming, a thousand miles to the northeast. The eleven million people in the Los Angeles metropolitan area are also dependent upon electricity that comes through four major power lines from as far away as New Mexico. The whole area is unnatural and isolated, almost totally dependent on long-drawn-out and extremely vulnerable lifelines from outside.

Metropolitan Los Angeles has the largest water transmission complex in the world. Three great aqueducts currently supply the area. The California Aqueduct, the longest in the world, brings water 500 miles from northern California rivers. Another brings water 338 miles from the Owens valley down the east side of the Sierra Nevada mountains. The third brings water 300 miles westward from the Colorado River, the tributaries of which extend another 700 miles deep into New Mexico, Utah, Colorado, and Wyoming. All of these supplies culminate in an extensive network of reservoirs along the aqueduct courses on the outskirts of, and within, the city, which itself owns more than a hundred reservoirs. This immense, intricate system is highly vulnerable at just about any point, whether from bacteriological or chemical agents, or demolition charges and other instruments.

In September, 1976, the California Aqueduct was dynamited, 200 miles north of Los Angeles. That immediately stopped the flow of 80 per cent of the city's water supply. It had been done, this time, by malcontented farmers because irrigation water was being diverted. The stoppage was brief. But had it been done by terrorists in several areas or at more critical junctures, the stoppage would have been lengthy and caused chaos.

Complicating this whole situation is a planned 5- to 12-billion-dollar nuclear power plant, the world's largest, which would generate enough electricity for five million people. The San Joaquin Nuclear Project, a joint undertaking of the L.A. Department of Water and Power (the nation's largest municipal utility) and the Southern California Edison and the Pacific Gas and Electric (two of the nation's largest power companies), was to be located north of Los Angeles in Kern County, an arid region requiring 20 billion gallons of water a year for cooling, that was to be obtained from the California Aqueduct. But if that water is denied, either through drought or terrorist-assisted interdiction, then those same five million people will be without power. Considering the terrain they traverse, there is no possible way that such water supply systems can be protected.

The same problems exist for electrical power. Thousands of miles of high tension lines traversing difficult terrain cannot be protected. Even within the metropolitan area they are quite vulnerable. Several years ago the journal *Black Politics* urged its readers to sabotage such lines, and described in detail how to do it easily, with a weapon as minimal as a .22 rifle. (The same journal urged and described how to sabotage a train carrying nerve gas so that it would drift over a major metropolitan area, a moon rocket as it was about to be launched, helicopter plants, napalm plants, and arms depots in metropolitan areas, among other things.) The utter inability to protect such lines was demonstrated by the sabotage incidents in Oregon.

Pentagon studies have been divulged establishing that the explosion of a supertanker loaded with oil or liquefied natural gas could easily kill 50,000. It would erupt with the force of a small A-bomb, devastating any nearby populated area. Again, a major secondary effect would be the consequent mass panic. It would also probably interdict the supply of fuel by destroying necessary port and storage facilities, which would be a third major effect. What would it require to wreak such havoc? Not much. A SAM rocket, mortar, a recoilless cannon. Thousands of such weapons have been stolen from U.S. military arsenals or are readily available on the international arms market. Many terrorist groups are already well equipped with such weapons. Merely downing a few airliners with SAMs as they make their approaches to Kennedy Airport in New York would devastate those highly populated areas.

Similarly, there are key junctures for telephone communications and pipelines. It has been divulged to the public that if a key grounding point in Utah is destroyed, it will put out of commission all telephone communications in the western U.S. If this were done in conjunction with an induced power blackout, the chaos would be indescribable. Even on a lesser scale the suspicious (and never explained) fire in Bell System's New York City central office in 1976 interrupted service in Manhattan for three weeks and caused an estimated 100-million-dollar loss for 10,000 small businesses.

Our major seaports and transportation centers are also huge unprotected targets of opportunity for serious disruption or destruction with minimal effort. Through them every day pass trucks, trains, and ships laden with oil, gas, explosives, kepone-type insecticides, propane gas, chemicals, and other lethal materials. The critical bridges, rail lines, canals, harbors, rivers, airports, and highways can be easily neutralized by sunken ships, auto accidents, or explosions. None of them is guarded. In the winter of 1976, for example, one sunken ship blocked the sea lane exit from the Great Lakes, causing hundreds of ships to be trapped and unable to leave before the winter storms and freeze.

There are also what are termed stationary "bombs." The sewage systems of hospitals and other facilities (located in densely populated areas) are highly volatile, it has recently been discovered. Indeed, they are likely to go up without any "inducement." Recently there was a massive explosion in a waste disposal area on Long Island, caused, it was thought, by a firecracker tossed by children. Other unguarded or little-guarded "bombs" include nuclear waste areas, chemical plants, oil and gas refineries, and storage areas.

The interdiction of key pipeline complexes in Ohio would cause the loss of a large part of the oil supply in the U.S., and in Houston and Monroe, Louisiana, of the natural gas supply upon which American industry so heavily depends. The recently completed Alaska pipeline may be a major target for terrorists in the future, especially in the event of another boycott or grave energy shortage. One Alaska state official has been quoted as describing the 800-mile-long pipeline as "the biggest target in the world for some nut" or "dedicated terrorists." One study concluded that during the long Arctic winter it would be impossible to defend. If ruptured at any one of twelve key junctures, its flow of heated oil would halt. Unless resumed within three weeks, the oil within the pipeline would, according to some experts, congeal into a hard, waxlike substance, becoming "the world's longest chapstick." It would take at least a year to clean out the pipeline. The estimate is based on the experience of the USSR when one of its pipelines ruptured in Siberia. In 1978 this pipeline was carrying 10 per cent of domestic U.S. production.

Questioned about some of these possibilities in an interview in *U.S. News & World Report* (June 20, 1977) Edward S. Patton, chairman of Alyeska Pipeline Service Company, denied that it would "freeze hard like a candle, but it can get to a jellylike consistency. The probability of such a thing happening is very small." Though the probability of its happening through an accident may be small, it is rather higher as a result of terrorism. In fact, it depends only on whether a terrorist wants to do it. In reply to a question about the recent report that it is highly vulnerable to sabotage, Patton avoided an answer: "Vandalism is always a problem. But the key, or critical, installations are protected." Terrorism, however, is something more than vandalism.

A major fire in May, 1977 in Saudi Arabia immediately forced the shutdown of 75 per cent of its oil production. Because the fire was confined to only one pumping station, the flow was restored within several days. Had it involved other pumping stations, the halt would have been much longer, and there would have been severe effects throughout the industrialized world. An Aramco spokesman ruled out the possibility of sabotage, suggesting that pipeline corrosion might have been responsible. However, there were initial reports of an explosion, and some media reports observed that there had been several major industrial fires in the eastern provinces of Saudi Arabia and in the neighboring Gulf States in recent weeks. A major secondary effect of the fire was that it caused a near panic on the Tokyo foreign currency and stock exchanges, despite assurances from the Japanese Government that the decrease in oil supply would be temporary. Japan imports 99 per cent of its oil, and 30 per cent from Saudi Arabia. Other world financial centers were also severely affected. Again, had the shutdown lasted longer, there would have been chaos in the international financial scene. One report that filtered out later from businessmen with contacts with Saudi officials said that informants had tipped off the Government that "Communist agents" had arrived in Saudi Arabia a month before the fire. It said that Arab and African Communists had been recruited for sabotage operations against Saudi Arabia, which is regarded as too pro-Western and conservative.

The fire disturbed even the *Times*. In its lead editorial, "The Fire Next Time," on Sunday, May 15, it posited the following scenario and then commented on it:

On Monday morning, June 13, 1977, the first effects of the Saudi Arabian pipeline fire began to be felt at the Exxon refinery at Baytown, N.J., and elsewhere in the United States. The summer driving season had, of course, already begun; the July 4 weekend was coming up fast. Without the fire, American refineries would have been turning out vast amounts of gasoline. The tankers that should have left Ras Tanura in May would, by then, have been disgorging their cargoes of crude oil. But because of the fire, they could not. So Baytown, like other refineries, had to go on what is called "allocation" — short rations. The real gasoline shortage fed public fears of an even worse one. The lines at gas stations grew longer. The sun bore down steadily, engines overheated, and, as a number of fistfights demonstrated, so did tempers.

Those scenes will not happen next month. The major Saudi oil fire that began Wednesday has been contained and production will resume imminently. Still, however imaginary the scenario, it is *imaginable*. As it was, first word of the fire sent shock waves through financial markets in Tokyo and drew headlines in the American press. Had the interruption been longer, the nation could have lost not only Saudi imports but others, too, under the share-the-loss emergency provisions of an international oil agreement. The shortage could have been even worse than that of the 1973-74 embargo.

So there is reason to be relieved — and plenty of reason to reflect again on the reality of the energy crisis against which

President Carter seeks to mobilize a still-skeptical public. There is little, short of rapid completion of a national oil stockpile, that his energy program could have done to allay the effects of a more serious fire now. But what about next year, or 1981, or 1985? How many close calls will be necessary for the public to understand the urgent need for a national energy program? The larger problem is not how to extinguish a fire in Saudi Arabia, but how to ignite one here.

The interconnection between energy and terrorism was — however inadvertently — brought into prominence by President Carter himself. In advance of his energy address in April, 1977, Carter's staff leaked two reports to the media. Jack Anderson described one of these as a "startling secret document" circulating inside the Carter Administration. Written by a "brilliant group of scientist-philosophers" headed by Dow Chemical's Jerry Decker and G. E.'s Dr. Willem Vedder, it warned that "social upheaval and revolution may destroy the U.S. by 2000 A.D." unless *drastic* steps are taken to solve the energy crisis. Cautioning against the foolhardy popular attitude that some technological miracle will rescue us at the last minute, it said that "there is not a straight-thinking scientist or engineer anywhere who can promise a new technological miracle of any kind . . . that will solve our energy problem."

As signaled to us by the Government and news media and the much-publicized Carter domestic "summit" (July, 1979), massive changes in the American lifestyle and enormously high taxes will be required to deal with the problem. Billions must be immediately expended on mining, transportation, and coal conversion projects. In regard to coal, upon which such heavy reliance has been placed, it warned that only 6 per cent of U.S. coal is now economically recoverable and that there is no way to transport it. As of now, to produce electricity from a billion tons would cost a staggering $310 billion. It urged that huge additional sums of money be spent for the development of gases, electricity, nuclear power, solar energy, and other forms of energy. Unless all these things are done simultaneously, the report concluded, "there is the very real possibility of this country slipping into an unimaginable catastrophe, with social upheaval and revolution not excluded."

Anderson, on the basis of "confidential" documents taken from the files of the ERDA, reported that that agency, which is charged with solving the nation's energy problem, was doing little or nothing. It was carrying on with a business-as-usual attitude even though the conclusions in one of its own documents, the "National Plan for Energy Research, Development and Demonstration," were the same as those of the Decker-Vedder group. Although couched in more soothing language, it too warned of revolution.

A second study leaked was the CIA report used by Carter in his address. In a highly unusual action that report was later made public officially by the White House — but only after his speech. It projected that in less than ten years (1985) world demand for oil would outstrip production. The result would be worldwide shortages and much higher prices for gas, fuel, and jet fuel, at least three times current prices. By 1990 gas would be two dollars a gallon, (but it is clear as of late 1979 that it is likely to rise to that level much sooner). It rejected the Interior Department's estimate that there are as many as one trillion barrels of undiscovered oil; it also seriously questioned current widespread estimates about how much proven reserves there are now.

Carter reputedly found the report "deeply disturbing." In his address to the nation he urged the "moral equivalent of war" to preclude a "national catastrophe." The news media, in accord with their self-justifying claims about keeping the citizens well informed, initially declined to provide live coverage of the speech. "We did not," a spokesman for a reluctant CBS-TV said, "think it warranted an interruption of our programming," i.e., soap operas and "film" stars playing game shows. And Ralph Nader of course disputed the study, seeing it as a conspiracy between the CIA and the oil companies to raise prices. Even William F. Buckley belatedly joined the chorus. The CIA report had also projected that the USSR would shift from being an exporter to a major importer of oil by 1985. About a month later the AP reported that the USSR, the world's largest oil producer, had approached the Iranian Government about the possibility of importing oil.

A third study, *Energy: Global Prospects 1985-2000,* conducted by MIT under the direction of Professor Carroll L. Wilson, was released on May 16, 1977. Its theme was similar to the CIA report: There is grave danger of an oil shortage by the 1980's, soaring fuel prices, and economic depression for industrial and developing nations. But the tone used by the MIT study was much grimmer than Carter's. Energy, it concluded, could "become a focus for confrontation and conflict.... Even with prompt action the margin between success and failure in the 1985-2000 period is slim."

Democratic governments, alas, have never been noted for prompt action. At a news conference Wilson elaborated on the 291-page report. He explained that 1985 was chosen because there was little that could be done before then to increase energy supplies. "Large investments and long lead times," he said, "are required to fill the prospective shortages." The report was based on studies by thirty-five principal participants from universities, corporations, and the U.S. and foreign governments. It pointed also to an additional problem resulting from increased reliance on nuclear energy: "No means of rendering plutonium useless for [nuclear] weapons is known." Moreover, even if Saudi Arabia doubles its present production, for which it has no incentive, since it can't spend the money it has now and would only be depleting its main resource, which it could sell in the future at much higher prices, it is only a question of time, the study argued, before a major oil shortage, 1989 at the latest.

As grimly pessimistic as these studies are, the projections are based on only what will happen if matters develop normally. They do not take into account the geometrically magnified effects should terrorism be added to the picture. The injection of the catalyst of technological terrorism into the projections would make these reports seem optimistic. The destruction of oil and gas pipelines and storage depots, power lines and stations, nuclear plants, water systems, port facilities, and others, would produce chaos of unimaginable proportions. The cost and the manpower to attempt to provide security for such vital installations is beyond estimate. It required $100 million, for example, to provide security for merely a few weeks at the Montreal Olympic Games.

What would happen if such terrorist interdictions of our energy and energy-related industries, especially food production and distribution, occurred? Few scientific studies have been made. Perhaps the study that gives the best *hint* of what might be in the offing is the Pentagon-commissioned research project NES (the National Entity Survival Studies) following the East Coast power blackout in 1965. A tiny relay failed in a Canadian power station and, within minutes, thirty million people were affected. Subways, trains, and elevators stopped. Radio and TV stations went off the air. The latter quickly returned as they switched to emergency generators, as did hospitals and a few other facilities. Street and traffic lights went out. Water pumps stopped.

But many things did not happen that would happen if something of that nature were terrorist-induced. Telephones, radio, and TV remained in operation and helped prevent mass panic. The area was less dependent on computers for a wide variety of essential functions than it is today. There was a full moon at the time, and the weather was relatively mild. Most people assumed it was only a brief stoppage, and it was. Supposing, however, communications had also been knocked out, the blackout had lasted for several days or weeks, and food, water, transistor batteries, candles, fuel for generators had run out — in such circumstances, the NES study concluded, panic and pandemic violence would have taken over. The police and other emergency services would have been unable to control the ensuing havoc.

During the 1965 blackout order and good will happily prevailed. This was not so during New York's second major blackout on July 14, 1977. It was for many a nightmare affair. Lawlessness reigned full sway from almost the first moment. Looting and arson were widespread and continued far into the following day. Thousands of false alarms added to the fire department's problems. Stores, banking, and Wall Street were badly disrupted. Property damage was costly and, for many small businesses, even ruinous. Over a hundred policemen were injured in their attempts to check the pillage and rioting. Close to 3,000 arrests were made — a fraction of the violators — which immobilized the city's criminal justice system for weeks. More than 75 million gallons of raw sewage bypassed New York City treatment plants during the power outage and were discharged directly into city waters, jeopardizing beaches on Long Island's North and South shores as well as city and Jersey shore areas. Governor Carey refused to call in the National Guard, on the ground that it would enflame the situation, since its men were not trained to deal with riots. Mayor Beame, as late as 2:30 A.M., was complaining indignantly on the radio that reports of looting were greatly exaggerated. At least one TV commentator openly justified the looting while it was in progress, attributing it to unemployment.

C.L. Sulzberger glumly summed it all up in his column in the *Times:*

> Nothing demonstrates how fragile modern society has become more than the gloomy drumbeat of statistical evidence accompanied by a counterpoint of occasional disasters like this month's blackout of New York. . . . What can happen to the structure of daily life in such circumstances was amply displayed when New York became a city of the dreadful night. It is appallingly evident to Americans and to technically advanced people everywhere that they no longer know how to exist without assured and uninterrupted flows of energy.

Had terrorists instigated and commandeered the blackout — as they very easily could have — the results would have been catastrophic. Terrorist gang members masquerading as policemen would have added brutality and carnage to the lawlessness that gained the upper hand for a while. By spreading rumors of food and water poisoning they would have provoked general panic. That they were not involved on this particular occasion is small comfort in view of subsequent, if lesser, "counterpoints" that *were* deliberate and calculated.

A month and a half later, on August 29, the UPI reported that Sausalito, California, "was blacked out early today when a series of explosions, apparently touched off by terrorist saboteurs, blew up an electrical substation . . . . It was one of the more damaging acts of sabotage against the power company of terrorists' attacks dating back nine years that have caused millions of dollars in damage and have left one man dead."

On March 8, 1978, the AP reported that an explosion at a power plant left a wide area of San Diego County without power, affecting about 400,000 persons. The entire North Island Naval Air Station was also without power.

On June 15, 1978, *The New York Times* reported that terrorists had detonated a chain of time bombs in a power plant on the outskirts of Rome, touching off a large fire that caused an estimated $600,000 worth of damage and leaving part of the city without power for several hours. Another powerful bomb was planted in front of the National Telephone Company in another part of the city, but the terrorists fled without setting the fuse when they were spotted by guards. A few weeks earlier they had also attempted to bomb a computer center.

On October 16, 1978, the AP reported that an explosion at a power station knocked out electric power in San Antonio and much of South Texas, necessitating the declaration of a state of emergency in San Antonio.

In November, 1978, Marxist terrorists in El Salvador blew up an electric plant and blacked out large sections of the capital.

On November 11, 1978, the *Los Angeles Times* reported that "three of the world's largest electric generators have been sabotaged at Grand Coulee Dam, keystone of the Pacific Northwest Power system, in a series of mysterious incidents that could cost the Federal Government millions of dollars. . . . The FBI confirmed that it was investigating the 'wilful damage'. . . . A Government source said circumstances suggest it was an inside job. . . . Another project spokesman said an instrument such as a small crowbar or chisel apparently was used." One generator would be out of commission for at least three months. The facility supplied power to Oregon, Washington, Idaho, Montana, and California.

Earlier in 1978 (February 18) the UPI reported that terrorists and other criminals in the U.S. have little difficulty obtaining explosives from construction sites, mines, and even military bases. Calling explosives control "a shambles," the Senate Judiciary Committee's Subcommittee on Criminal Laws and Procedures urged a complete overhaul of explosives control laws and more stringent penalties for violations. It said large quantities of explosives were stolen from poorly guarded storage areas at construction sites, mines, and elsewhere, including military bases. It concluded that "the regulations and the machinery of control are so flawed that virtually anyone, given a degree of initiative, can purchase virtually any quantity of explosives for any purpose."

As of 1979 adequate safeguards are still lacking. There is next to nothing to prevent a determined gang of terrorists from having a field day anywhere at any time they choose.

2. Andromeda Strains

TO MANY experts the prospect of biological terrorism is the most frightening of all. There are certainly many interesting little things that even high school students can develop in their own school laboratories. We recall also the threat made by the Baader-Meinhof gang to spread anthrax through the mails of West Germany. But the area of gene engineering offers really exciting prospects for the development of megadeath weapons. The debate in this area has been limited almost completely to the normal dangers (which are enormous) that obtain from such research. Only a few scientists have dealt with this matter as related to the problem of terrorism. And in the professional literature on terrorism, no one has, as far as we know, discussed the danger. Only Lowell Ponte has called attention to the great potential this research has for the development of race-specific weapons.

In a front-page article in the *Times* (May 16, 1976) Boyce Rensberger ("Debate on Shifting Genes Nearing a Critical Phase") reported that:

biologists, who have recently discovered the potentially revolutionary technique for creating new forms of life, believe they have acquired such a fundamental power, promising great benefits to society and threatening massive disaster, that they face major ethical dilemmas.

He compared them to the similar dilemmas of the nuclear physicists of a generation ago. Such techniques make it possible to select genes from one organism and transplant them into the chromosomes of another. Significantly, most of the researchers are using bacteria as the recipient species. Although the debate over the prudence of such research had been going on for several years, the National Institutes of Health Services still had not promulgated any official guidelines for the containment of such research to prevent bacterial escapes. Scientific critics warned that such escapes could produce epidemics or massive disruptions of ecological balances. According to the article, most experts agreed that the obviously hazardous experiments involving known, highly virulent disease organisms, for example, should not be attempted for the present. It appears, Rensberger said, that only one major academic research center, the University of Michigan, has even considered the pros and cons at its highest administrative levels. He then described that debate at Michigan in some detail, quoting one scientist there as saying "despite everything you've heard, nobody really knows the kind of risks that are involved."

About a week later the AP reported that "a controversial type of genetic research, capable of creating new life forms and considered potentially dangerous by its critics, has received the go-ahead from the University of Michigan regents." It stated that Michigan was the first university to give formal consent to the experiment.

Three weeks later, the *Times* described at length the "heated dispute" at Harvard over research in this area:

A biologist who works near the planned project wants his office moved. The Mayor of Cambridge says that he fears that the professors may produce a "monster." But the scientists who want to carry out the experiment with government money, while conceding that they do not know what might happen, say they will be very, very careful. . . . But opponents are warning that the experiments could cause unknown diseases — diseases that could be transmitted but not diagnosed or treated. . . . Dr. George Wald, the 1967 Nobel Prize winner for biology, urged the mayor to try to block the planned genetic research laboratory. . . .

The experiments are to be financed through a grant of about five hundred thousand dollars from the National Institutes of Health. The major condition is the construction of a special safety laboratory, designated as P-3, slightly less secure than what the Army uses for its chemical and biological warfare experiments. The vehicle for the experiments is a common form of bacteria known as E-coli. . . . Critics of the proposal, like Ruth Gordon, biology professor, called the experiments a health hazard because no one knows what can happen, and possible diseases could easily be carried from the laboratory to the crowded city. But Francis M. Pipkin, an Associate Dean who chaired one of the review committees, told the Harvard *Crimson:* "There is no evidence from which to decide. It's never been done before, so we don't know its consequences. There's no reason to think it's ultradangerous." His committee unanimously approved the project.

On July 8 the Cambridge City Council voted to establish a three-month "good faith" moratorium and study period for the matter. One of those who spoke in opposition to the research was "a former laboratory technician at Cambridge's Massachusetts Institute of Technology, who said he had quit his job after he observed 'safety standards constantly violated, either by carelessness or accidents in the research lab.' "

On July 12 *U.S. News and World Report* published a major article on the subject under the heading "Science's

Newest 'Magic' — A Blessing or a Curse?" The article pointed out that genetic modifications are haphazard and can take hundreds of thousands of years to evolve and that the evolutionary process can now be preempted with a precision undreamed of just five years ago:

> But there is a dark side as well, a nightmarish potential to create by mistake laboratory "monsters" that might accidentally be unleashed on society. These modern Frankenstein creations most probably would be "super" bacteria, resistant to drugs and causing new kinds of diseases rather than curing the illnesses that they had been created to combat. The revolutionary discoveries that are making genetic engineering possible are barely three years old, but their use has generated one of the hottest scientific debates of the century. . . . On one side was the chairman of the board of Miles Laboratories, Walter Ames Compton, who said: "We must hold that scientific investigation must never be permanently halted in the face of hazardous potential. . . . We further hold that only ignorance, not knowledge, has been shown repeatedly in history to be the real danger of mankind." The debate is a rarity in the annals of modern science because the issue of risk and hazards was initially raised by the very scientists who were most deeply embroiled in the research. . . At a meeting in California in February, 1975, now known as the Asilomar Conference, David Baltimore, a Nobel Prize-winning cancer researcher, told the group: "We're here because a new technology of molecular biology appears to have allowed us to abort the standard events of evolution by making combinations of genes that could be unique in natural history. These pose special hazards while they offer enormous benefits. . . . Most of the work in this field has involved use of a bacterium called E coli. . . . If some E coli bacteria are genetically altered for an experiment, they might find ready environment in which to flourish in a lab technician or scientist who inhaled or ingested them. The experimenter inadvertently could carry the bacteria out of the laboratory in his body — a common occurrence in even the best labs — and

contaminate people outside. . . . The cause could remain unknown for years, and the disease would respond to no known drugs. Three approaches are being developed to prevent this kind of contamination — physical containment, biological containment, and outright prohibition of some types of research. Physical containment means putting barriers between bacteria and scientists. Some laboratories that use a high degree of physical containment for other research are notoriously sloppy about procedures. Experimental strains of bacteria and viruses, for example, have been dumped down the laboratory sink. With some mutated strains of bacteria created by genetic engineers, society could not afford this kind of mistake, in the view of scientists working in the fields. [Biological containment means] developing strains of E coli that cannot survive in a salty environment, such as the one found in the human body. [It also means developing a strain] that dies when it comes into contact with the detergents that are found in any sewer in America. This kind of biological shielding makes experimental E coli a poor bet to survive outside the protective laboratory environment. A problem with biological containment, however, is caused by a quirk of nature. Even though scientists can almost guarantee that experimental bacteria will not survive for long outside the laboratory, they cannot guarantee that the DNA molecules that are part of the genes of the dead bacteria will not be absorbed by a living cell. . . . So there is a potential for pass along. Even if the prime carrier of a mutated gene dies, the genetic message can still be perpetuated in rare cases. Thus, there is no fail-safe way to protect society from by-products of genetic engineering. What can be done, and is being done, is to reduce that exposure to the lowest possible level. A major concern of the critics is the expected proliferations of laboratories working in this field. There are now several dozen such research centers around the world. The number is expected to run into the hundreds in the next few years — each creating its own form of hybrid life and increasing a chance of a deadly mistake. . . . Ultimately, it will be the scientists themselves who decide the issue. Observers are asking: Are the people deeply involved in this research the best judges of whether their work harbors more risk than society should be asked to bear?

Liebe F. Cavalieri, a member of Sloan-Kettering Institute for Cancer Research and professor of biochemistry at Cornell University Graduate School of Medical Sciences, gave a resounding no to that question in a major article in *The New York Times Magazine* (August 22, 1976).

Many of the most prominent scientists in the field are clearly frightened over what may result from the normal course of research, even if all of the so-called "safeguards" were to be (voluntarily) adhered to. Such "safeguards," of little concern to scientists, would have no value at all against terrorists.

The measures taken by the U.S. Government are virtually nonexistent. The *Washington Post* reported (September 23, 1976) that U.S. health officials acknowledged that the Government does not even know "what companies are trying to create revolutionary new forms of life, or the whereabouts of their laboratories. Several senators expressed distress over the disclosure, emphasizing that no one knows for certain whether recombinant DNA research, also called genetic engineering, promises unlimited benefits such as life-saving new drugs and agricultural products, or a 'biological holocaust.' " NIH director Frederickson was quoted as testifying that "nearly all" affected Federal agencies have said they would comply "voluntarily" with the NIH guidelines.

Science magazine, a professional journal, also raised serious questions about the research in an article in its October 15, 1976, issue, and comments on it in the January 14, 1977, issue. It was pointed out that NIHS and other Government agencies had engaged in massive violations of the law, in particular the National Environmental Policy Act (NEPA) of 1969. According to that law, alternative policies for DNA technology were supposed to have been under consideration in the fall of 1976. The *Science* article stated: "The nuclear genie is now out of the bottle for good or ill, and the crucial time of grace for instituting control over the recombinant DNA technique is probably over." A "moratorium" agreed to in July, 1974, had suspended work on two types of experiments, but merely advised caution on a third — the insertion of animal genes in bacteria — and so work in that area went ahead. At the Asilomar conference the moratorium was ended and replaced by broad guidelines for all experiments except those of the highest risk. The most disturbing aspect of the whole thing is that a handful of Nobel Prize-seeking scientists are making these decisions completely on their own, playing Russian roulette with all our lives.

A correspondent to *Science,* with some understatement, described the enormous dangers:

> The situation is troubling because . . . two mechanisms should have ensured a more careful approach to formation of policy for genetic manipulation. First, the original charge to the NIH guidelines committee required that research aimed at defining the risks precede the development of guidelines. . . In fact, the reverse procedure has occurred. Secondly, in violation to NEPA, the NIH reversed the order of procedure and sanctioned a policy of proliferation prior to formal consideration of that policy under the laws.

The prudent safeguard against premature or ill-considered actions that pose significant environmental hazards has, the article noted, by accident or design, been circumvented. And most important,

> if recombinant DNA techniques prove as powerful as expected and human nature and hardware as unreliable as they have always been, proliferation is almost certain to have disastrous consequences eventually. But to establish a policy

of proliferation by default is not only to uncork the genetic genie in a manner likely to bring about disaster: it is also to deny the public its right to make an informal decision on a matter which vitally affects its interests.

The article called for a moratorium until policy options have been considered and chosen through democratic procedures, even though it would be frustrating to scientists who make demands in the name of freedom of inquiry.

In January, too, Dr. Cavalieri appeared before two Assembly committees of the California legislature and warned that there was not only a danger of releasing some unstoppable disease-causing organism, but also a possibility of terrorists' obtaining some and blackmailing society. That was one of the few warnings about the possibilities of DNA technology for terrorism.

The two largest enviromental law firms in the nation, the Environmental Defense Fund and the Natural Resources Defense Council, also filed a petition to the Department of Health, Education, and Welfare. They argued that voluntary compliance is inadequate and that private industry is not covered at all by the NIH guidelines.

But by this time the major pressure groups for the pro-genetic research scientists had geared up for a great struggle in behalf of "science" and "freedom." They opposed "the strict guidelines" issued by NIH. They trotted out all the old chestnuts about Galileo and the "freedom of inquiry" established by the Renaissance. They enlisted powerful men in their cause. George W. Ball, for example, described the threatened constraints in terms of a "new medieval church." Others argued that unrestrained science is the "key to our political future." A researcher at Cold Spring Harbor, Long Island, dismissed all the opponents as "kooks" and "incompetents" (*The New York Times,* May 15, 1977), an odd way of characterizing Nobelists and scientists with the qualifications of Cavalieri, himself a pioneer in the area.

They were successful in preventing any significant regulation. As *Newsday* summed it up in a lengthy backgrounder (February 16, 1977), "regulation of DNA research remains essentially a matter of good faith." Nobody even seemed to know how many institutions and corporations were engaged in the technology. If they want Government money, they merely register and "promise" to follow NIH guidelines. In April, for example, the New York City Health Department revealed that there were no restraints on the research in the city. There were now, it said, "many" such experiments being conducted within the city.

As in the case of nuclear power, we have the constant invocation that "strict safeguards" are in force when in fact next to nothing is in force. And we have, too, the utter lack of concern about the public safety, especially from the standpoint of technological terrorism.

3. Computers

OUR increasingly computer-based technology is an area that promises to be especially fertile for terrorist operations. It too is an area that has received only scant attention in this respect, no doubt because it lacks the cataclysmic bang of a nuclear bomb or the spectacle of millions dying from some virulent bacillus. If the general rule is that the vulnerability of a nation or a metropolitan area is roughly proportional to its centralization, then the potential for havoc in this area is enormous. Donn B. Parker, for example, emphatically warned in his *Crime by Computer* that "programmers and others in sensitive electronic data processing [E.D.P.] jobs are potentially the most dangerous people in the world."

Although Parker, a senior information processing analyst at Stanford Research Institute, deals almost exclusively with the problem from the standpoint of crime for monetary gain, barely mentioning terrorism, those same vulnerabilities can be utilized even more effectively for political destabilization. As Carlos Marighela candidly emphasized in his *Minimanual of the Urban Guerrilla*, the terrorist does the very same things as the criminal but for different purposes. Since negotiable assets are increasingly represented by electronic pulses and magnetic patterns stored in computers and squirted through telephone lines, organized and white-collar crime will naturally focus on where those negotiable assets are. Parker describes a number of possible threat scenarios. One is the sudden unavailability of data processing capabilities resulting from sabotage or other causes. Computers are very delicate, and they can easily be destroyed or put out of operation by using instruments as simple as a hammer, water, or gasoline.

The physical security and well-being of people are also becoming more and more dependent on the reliable and uninterrupted functioning of computers, such as the operation of mass transit systems in large metropolitan areas, nuclear facilities, monitoring of patients in hospital intensive care wards, traffic control, telephone and other communications, electric power supply, water, and air traffic control, to mention but a few. Many, perhaps most, have no backup systems or duplicate tapes. Computers are also extensively used in the two key areas of government and business.

There are, according to Parker's figures, some 150,000 computers in use in the United States, and by 1980 the total will be over 500,000. Most of them are being used directly in the processing of wealth and information. Equally significant, from the standpoint of prospects for a "garrison state," is the estimate of Stanford Research Institute that in 1975 2,230,000 people were working directly with computers (about 3 per cent of the 82 million work force), and the estimate in a report issued by the American Federation of Information Processing and *Time* magazine that 7 per cent of the work force claimed they worked directly with computers as long ago as 1971. Using only those dated figures, the opportunity for 3 to 7 per cent of the work force to perpetrate financial and informational chaos, whether for criminal or terrorist purposes, is indeed terrifying. Writing as one of the most respected experts in the area of computer security, Parker warns that as of now "no practical way has been devised to audit the work of these people sufficiently because of the increasing complexity of computer systems and the lack of standards, disciplines, and structured practices in their design and construction."

Since computer abuse is infrequently mentioned in works on terrorism, and since Parker deals with the subject in regard to crime and negligence alone, it is worth summarizing briefly the major points and conclusions of his analysis, but from the standpoint here of political terrorism. The effects of computer abuse for that purpose will be greatly magnified because the terrorist has fewer qualms and restraints than does the criminal. His goal is not to use the system to obtain money, rather the very destruction of the system itself.

Basically, tactical terrorism through computers can be done in two ways: when the computer is the target and when it is the instrument of the operation. The first method would involve its destruction or temporary denial of use through sabotage. The second would involve altering the tapes, making it lie or do something it is not supposed to do. In regard to the latter, Parker points out that since data stored in computers are highly volatile and time-sensitive, the slightest alteration in a program or any stray pulse of electrical current could result in the data being erased forever. This type would require people who have the requisite skills, knowledge, resources, and access. But this expertise is, increasingly, widely available in our society. And much more so than most of us realize. For some inexplicable reason, the social engineers seem to have hit upon computer skills as the be-all and end-all vocational training to solve the problems of the "disadvantaged," the disaffected, the marginally employed, and — incredibly — convicts. Give such people a nice technological skill, and we shall solve an enormous social problem, we are told.

As Parker observes, the expected sources of potential perpetrators are trivial compared with the many more successful white-collar and professional criminals with opportunities for E.D.P. education in high schools, trade schools, in-service training programs, and colleges. Moreover, professional criminals are rapidly obtaining the requisite expertise, whether through prison training schools or computer trade schools. Ironically — or imprudently — the Federal Government sponsors such programs in Federal penal institutions in the interest of rehabilitation. Even more incredible, several of the major computer manufacturers have established programs at various prisons, including maximum security ones. Honeywell, for example, has long had a program at Walpole State Prison in Massachussetts. Trained ex-convicts are then normally hired into sensitive computer jobs. According to Parker, they have had an unusually good record. But he warns that they are especially subject, for obvious reasons, to extortion and pressure.

However, from the standpoint of terrorism, there are additional factors to assess that Parker does not consider because he is concerned only with criminals. In discussing the prison program, he stresses that only the most carefully screened and best-motivated prisoners are admitted. But would it be possible to deny such "educational training" to "model prisoners" if they insist on it, especially if they are black or from some other "ethnically disadvantaged" group and, as may well be the case, have the backing of the ACLU? Not likely, no matter how violently revolutionary they may be. Parker is clearly unaware of the rather substantial body of literature demonstrating that prisons have become, in effect, "boot-camps" for revolutionaries. As long ago as 1969 twenty-six states were offering E.D.P. in prisons.

But for terrorist action to destroy or deny temporarily the use of certain computers, computer expertise is not necessary. Only certain terrorist skills, and often quite minimal ones, are needed, and this is another aspect of the problem Parker does not analyze. A bomb, a fire, the denial of electricity or telephone circuits, or even a hammer would be sufficient.

What Parker does provide us with is an analysis of the problem of security — which is enormous — though merely from the standpoint of crime for financial gain. Computer security entails safeguards systems in three basic areas: physical security for the building and the computer facilities, including data communications and air-conditioning; operational and procedural security, which means constraints on employees; and internal computer security over the controls and protection mechanisms. But it involves even more than this in regard to terrorism, because those systems depend on electricity and telephone circuits that can easily be interdicted. According to Parker, however, perfect security is unobtainable, even against crime, to say nothing of terrorism. Thus far security technologists have attempted to deal with the problem by developing technical methods and devices. But that approach is misdirected. The security problem, Parker warns, is primarily one of people. The goal should be to reduce the number of people in positions of trust and to reduce the amount of trust it is necessary to place in them. Even so, there will always be a core of persons in the most sensitive areas: systems and applications programmers, maintenance engineers, data preparation technicians, and operators. If these people cannot be trusted, "then forget all the technical methods of computer security — they will be worthless." To achieve even a minimal degree of trust, however, we must add, would entail a major step toward the much-feared "garrison state."

Security for computers today, whether for internal operations or external attacks, is totally inadequate. Many organizations, Parker notes, are not even aware of the potential for losses or their high degree of vulnerability. Effective methods of deterrence, detection, prevention, and recovery have not yet been implemented or even discovered. The common procedure today is the "cookbook" method, which relies on functional checklists of safeguards. Unfortunately, Parker observes, this leads to a Maginot Line attitude. It is then merely necessary to "end-run" the safeguards, since the criminal is not using the same checklist. However, the criminal may well be using the same checklist, perhaps even using Parker's book, for the precise purpose of "end-running" the system. The prospective criminal or terrorist would no doubt thoroughly analyze those works Parker conveniently lists as the best in the area of security. As in the case of Taylor's work on nuclear theft, the warning is necessarily a primer.

Checklists are useful tools, Parker concludes, but they are not the answer to cost-effective security. A new method, threat scenario analysis, he advises, has been used with significant success at Stanford Research Institute. But that too, we should note, has the same problem with "people" security that Parker analyzes in regard to technological safeguards. In short, those very threat scenarios could be effectively used by someone desiring to compromise the system because of the lack of security for the threat scenarios.

The same situation we described at length in regard to nuclear security evidently prevails for computer security. The corporate, cost-effective mind, Parker observes, resists efforts to increase security. Since the system is already unbelievably complex, the idea of imposing an entire new level of complexity and constraints in the interest of security is seen as overwhelmingly impractical, expensive, and unnecessary. In fact, the insurmountable problem thus far, according to computer scientists, has been that no one has yet been able to design a computer system that is truly secure and, more important, could be proven to remain secure over the lifetime of the system. Without Congressional legislation to force the development of secure systems, he feels it is unlikely. But it must be made clear, he warns, "to the business community, the government, and finally the public that the safety of our economy and our society is growing increasingly dependent on the safe use of secure computers."

He describes in some detail what the ideally secure system should have so that it would be safe from compromise without human intervention, being served by operators who would be allowed to perform their functions under the direction of, and close monitoring by, the computer itself. The goal would be to make all failures failsafe. But again, he does not concern himself with the problem of damage from an external force. It might require, he speculates, four trusted executives, including a special Government inspector, to turn keys simultaneously to change the mode of operation from "secure" to "open." Only then would human access be allowed. Before restoring it to "secure," it would be necessary to have a team of auditors go through an elaborate process of doublechecking and testing the "secure" condition. Then, another group of four executives would simultaneously turn their keys to make it operable in the "secure" condition. It would also be necessary for the computer itself to monitor and control its physical environment. It must also control, as subsystems, the air-conditioning, fire detection and suppression equipment, personnel access, and periphery intrusion alarms.

Again we must point out that in the light of the number of computers now being used and of those that soon will be used in rather sensitive areas, such a secure system would entail a rather large number of people who must be "trusted." To establish that trust would require another major step in the direction of the national security state. As Parker points out, for example, much reliance is now being placed on auditors. But they are constrained to audit "around," since they know little about computer technology. They look at what goes in and what comes out, with no concern for what is happening inside the mysterious "black box." Between the auditors and the source documents are the programmers, tape librarians, operators, engineers, and systems programmers. The auditor is forced to trust all these people implicitly. He cannot, therefore, really audit.

The most that security practices can do today, Parker concludes, is to contain the problem. Even that, we think, is an optimistic assessment. It is not a matter of merely making some adjustments, however expensive such bandaids may be, in the computers. It requires an entirely new generation of computers with security programmed into them. To date, as described earlier, no such computers have been designed, much less built, probably because of cost-conscious corporate executives.

Parker and other computer security experts are clearly worried. Recognition of the threat and the development of methods to control it have been slow in coming, he believes, because of the natural tendency to wait until disaster befalls us before spending any funds on the problem.

The purpose of his book was to demonstrate that the problem could soon start to assume serious proportions. As in the case of nuclear security, nothing significant appears likely to be done until a major crisis occurs.

As if to reemphasize the central conclusions of Parker's analysis, a GAO study was made public in May, 1976, which concluded that many of the Federal Government's 9,000 computers are insufficiently protected against sabotage, vandalism, terrorism, or natural disaster. The GAO said it had found lax security practices at a number of Federal computer installations. Such practices make the installations especially susceptible to "losses caused by bombings, fires, floods, frauds, thefts, embezzlements and human errors." Senator Ribicoff, who released the report, said great havoc and personal inconvenience to Americans could result if, through the "government's failure to adequately protect computer facilities," tax, social security, or veterans' records were destroyed. According to the report, more than half of the installations visited were without plans for "continuity of operations if a loss occurred." The agency, according to the AP, declined to identify the centers, contending that it did not want to call the inadequate standards to the attention of would-be saboteurs. Certainly computer centralization makes it far easier today to destroy all the records of a given agency.

The Greer/Kandel Report (September 16, 1976) also revealed that "... terrorist groups are shifting their focus from the U.S. Government to American companies in this country as well as overseas, according to our sources in private security organizations, who have become increasingly worried about the development." It stated further that

> CIA officials are also worried about the security of such major installations as offshore drilling rigs, nuclear reactor sites, the computer that runs the Bay Area Rapid Transit System in San Francisco, and pipelines (including the Alaska

Pipeline). They fear that as terrorist incidents multiply, headline hunting groups . . . will resort to more spectacular acts of terrorism to give them the publicity they crave.

The *Washington Post* described in December, 1976, a growing concern within the Federal Government about computer abuse — for instance, getting information from National Institutes of Health computers to blackmail Government officials who have been hospitalized for mental reasons, or the use by potential assassins of Secret Service computers to learn if they are being watched. It went on to point out that computer espionage has also arrived on the scene. It described how the State Department "almost" expelled a Soviet diplomat who was recruiting employees of a computer manufacturer with access to Pentagon computers, and the ring of programmers in West Germany routinely siphoning government records from computers they serviced and selling them to East Germany. The *Post* quoted Parker as saying that of the 200,000 computers in use in the U.S., only 200 are rated as secure by experts, and these are the ones used by the National Security Agency, the FBI, the CIA, and the Pentagon. But "some computer experts aren't even sure about the machines at these agencies."

One of the computers those agencies use widely is Control Data's Cyber-76 — the Pentagon, for nuclear weapons targeting and other functions; the CIA and NSA, for processing of codes and intelligence data. And it is this computer that Control Data was in the process of selling to the Soviet Union. According to Jack Anderson, scarcely a hard-liner on matters of security, it would be turned against us to track U.S. missiles, planes, and submarines, and would be capable of decoding sensitive U.S. intelligence transmissions. It could also be used to improve the production of nuclear warheads, multiple-headed missiles, and other military hardware. Control Data, insisting it had provided "adequate safeguards," contemptuously dismissed opposition to the sale as coming from "conservatives," and as being based on "ill-informed hysteria," thereby fulfilling Lenin's prediction that when the time comes to hang the capitalists, they will fight among each other to "sell us the rope." One of the "adequate safeguards" upon which Control Data placed great stress was the requirement that two of its technicians be on the site twenty-four hours a day. In earlier instances the Kissinger-dominated National Security Council had overridden objections from the Pentagon and allowed Control Data to sell Cyber-73 computers to the USSR and China. The knowledge gained through possession of these computers could easily be used to compromise our own.

A major GAO report on the lack of safeguards for computers was issued in July, 1977. It found that the Social Security Administration's files on millions of Americans "are not properly safeguarded from potential loss, destruction, abuse or misuse." In general, it found four broad "security weaknesses" in the Government's massive computer systems. In one instance it found that "a private company built a flourishing business by gaining unauthorized access to Federal medical records and selling the information to many of the nation's insurance companies." It concluded:

> With a few exceptions, individual employees can gain access to the information in the files and even create new files without being required by the computer to identify themselves. . . . In many offices, computer and communication terminals are situated where virtually any Social Security Administration employee can operate them. Even in offices, where the terminals are situated in a single room, the agency found that access to terminal rooms was not restricted to selected, designated individuals.

In an earlier report (June, 1977) the GAO had criticized the lack of locks and personnel controls, and in effect had contradicted assurances given Congress more than six months earlier by the Social Security Administration. SSA Commissioner Wortman had informed Representative Moss (D. Calif.) that access to all communication rooms "is on a 'need to know' basis." He also contended, in contrast to the GAO findings, that every terminal of his agency's advanced computer system "is capable of being locked" by means of a code word program. At this time, significantly, Federal law did not even define computerized data as tangible property.

The almost complete absence of safeguards was described in a backgrounder in the *Times* (July 3, 1977):

> More than two million Americans have access to computers, and almost any one of them can penetrate electronic security systems that have been repeatedly documented to be lax. . . . Because of the very nature of a computer, the invader need not even go near it. All he needs is a keyboard terminal, much like an electric typewriter and a telephone. The thief merely dials the number of the computer he wishes to invade and uses the keyboard terminal to punch out the purloined password. The thief's knowledge of computer language and programs then allows him to order the machine to do his bidding, such as transferring corporate funds electronically to his personal bank account. Then he may even order the computer to erase the magnetic tracks of the transaction. The security of computers, or the abysmal lack of it, is being given increasing attention.

One expert declared that "illegal activities by legitimate users of computers are almost impossible to stop and are likely to remain so in the near future because defense mechanisms are extremely expensive." The *Times* referred to a Government report released earlier in 1977 detailing the Government's "inability to adequately secure its 10,000 computers against fraud, compromise and physical assault. This lack of adequate security is especially evident in those government computers which handle the distribution of public funds and those which hold economically valuable and privacy data." At this time Congress was holding hearings on proposed legislation. But Congress moves rather leisurely on these matters.

On March 7, 1978, the AP revealed that Congressional investigators, in testing the security of the SSA's national computer complex, had walked out recently with a cart carrying the names and addresses of 1.14 million beneficiaries. After acknowledging that the incident had occurred, agency officials once again said that corrective steps had been taken. The tapes were taken by GAO investigators. "They were boasting that they were completely secure, and we wanted to test and see," a GAO official said. "They were kind of embarrassed." The GAO told the Carter Administration that if criminals had stolen the tapes, adding to or altering the beneficiary list could have resulted in a massive fraud. Senator Ribicoff said: "This is probably the biggest civilian computer center in the world, and, frankly, I am shocked at such lax security." The GAO maintained that "the central computer facility is still not secure. Unauthorized personnel have access to the computer room and tape vault. We were able to remove both blank and valid cards from the central computer facility through both the security gates and the emergency exits." As in the other areas we have discussed, we find that here too we have repeated assurances from Government officials concerning stringent safeguards, which are, it is subsequently found, utterly untrue.

Representative Moss also revealed (July 29, 1977) that a report prepared by the Mitre Corporation for the White House Office of Telecommunications Policy, entitled "Selected Examples of Possible Approaches to Electronic

Communication Interception Operations," was in effect "a how-to-do-it manual on non-court-ordered wiretapping." Among other things it described in detail how to intercept data being exchanged between businesses and computer companies.

In October, 1977, computer scientists and mathematicians — whose research involved secret codes — protested what they described as harassment and the threat of sanctions by the National Security Agency, or even prosecution for publishing articles about their work. Scientists, some working for Universities, others for private industry, and some for the Federal Government, charged that research faces a muted but growing threat from the NSA. The *Times* blandly noted (October 19,1977) that "most computer scientists and mathematicians in the United States are members of the Institute of Electric and Electronic Engineers, which publishes their papers and distributes them to countries abroad, including the Soviet Union."

A week later *Newsday* reported (October 24, 1977) that that same institute somewhat inconsistently was charging that the NSA had pressured the Government into adopting deliberately inferior standards for encoding computer data, as a means of insuring the agency's capability of tapping into domestic computers if necessary. They said that the agency is exposing American computers to foreign spying by insisting on the low encoding standard for their protection. The article noted that an estimated $30 billion is transferred daily by computer. In addition, much important intelligence information involving economics moves over computer terminals or is stored in data banks. The computers can be tapped like any telephone line.

By early 1978 there was much discussion about the computer chip revolution, "miracle" chips developed through microtechnology that will transform society. A chip the size of a thumbnail has the calculating capability of a room-size computer of only twenty-five years ago. In a lengthy cover story *Time* magazine (February 20, 1978) described it as a "quantum leap in the technology of mankind, a development that over the past few years has acquired the force and significance associated with the development of hand tools or the discovery of the steam engine." However, it also noted that many scientists are quite apprehensive:

Dr. D. Raj Reddy, a computer scientist at Pittsburgh's Carnegie-Mellon University, fears that universally available microcomputers could turn into formidable weapons. Among other things, says Reddy, sophisticated computers in the wrong hands could begin subverting a society by tampering with people's relationships with their own computers — instructing the other computers to cut off telephone, bank and other services, for example. The danger lies in the vast expanding computer data banks, with their concentration of information about people and governments, and in the possibility of access to those repositories. Already, computer theft is a growth industry, so much so that the FBI has a special program to train agents to cope with the electronic cutpurse. . . . These versatile machines have become the galley slaves of capitalism. Without them, the nation's banks would be buried under the blizzard of 35 billion checks that rain down on them annually.

The movement toward complete centralized computerized banking and electronic fund transfers (EFT's) is highly disturbing in terms of possible terrorist disruption. In major articles in late May and early June, 1977, in the *Wall Street Journal*, *The New York Times*, and *Fortune*, the development was seen as all but inevitable. The Congressionally established National Commission on Electronic Fund Transfers recommended that Government rules be changed to encourage the nationwide spread of

EFT's. One of the prime movers in its behalf has been Citibank. Parker has described in his work the chaos that ensued when one small bank was denied the use of its computer for a day or so. People do, it seems, get rather panicky when they cannot obtain their money. An institution the size of Citibank, however, is another story. It has also conveniently located its main computer, upon which the others depend, in Huntington, Long Island. It is difficult to imagine the chaos that would ensue if some enterprising terrorist were to knock out that computer when EFT has been fully established. All it would require is a SAM rocket, a small force of attackers, or any of several other rather minimal terrorist instruments. Terrorist manuals, it should be noted, commonly stress that the best way to attack capitalism is to attack its nervous system, the banking network. Bankers, by centralizing computers and by failing to provide even trivial security, are making that task ludicrously easy. How easy was demonstrated in October, 1978, when a computer consultant used his expertise to steal $10.2 million from a California bank — simply by making a single phone call.

Insurance companies too, like all progressive corporations, are busily engaged in putting everything on computer tapes, that is, centralizing their information. Again, no one has, to our knowledge, discussed the exciting potential they have for terrorist purposes. In *A Man Called Intrepid*, however, Sir William Stephenson is quoted in explaining their value for sabotage operations: "If you have access to insurance company files, you will see detailed studies of the weak point in any manufacturing process or mining procedure. Insurance companies stand to lose fortunes from an accident, and so they employ experts to figure out every possible way that things can go wrong. Their reports are guidebooks for saboteurs." Since then, however, things have been made easier through computers. But whether computerized or not, those files have only minimal security from the standpoint of sophisticated terrorist groups or in regard to the possibilities for compromising, through blackmail or extortion, members of their rather large work forces.

In mid-1978 Thomas Whiteside's *Computer Capers* appeared. Originally a series of articles in *The New Yorker*, it depended heavily upon Donn B. Parker's *Crime By Computer*, as the *Business Week* (July 3, 1978) reviewer noted. He said further that this is a major problem for various Government defense agencies where computers hold national secrets.

> In one exercise to determine how good the security was for an Air Force computer, two security consultants were able to penetrate its operating system in two hours. All they used were their expert knowledge of how computers work and a keyboard terminal connected to a home telephone. If the terminal had, for example, been connected to a phone in Moscow, the men would have been able to crack open the computer in the same way.

The review of the book in the Sunday *Times* concluded: "The computer has not yet been designed that cannot be penetrated or sabotaged. The abuses have been rampant; the disasters, as Mr. Whiteside demonstrates, may be waiting to happen." Whiteside's parting words are worth heeding:

> Whether in the military, in government, or in business, the designers of currently contemplated computer systems seem no more able to promise absolute solutions to the problem of data security than chess players are able to foresee games in which White can never be beaten. And in the meantime, nobody knows what Trojan-horse programs might be lying in wait in computer systems until at the appropriate signal, they spill out in acts of disruption and pillage.

The Gallagher President's Report, A Confidential Letter to Chief Executives (October 11, 1978) ominously reported the findings of a poll of a hundred company presidents on corporate security. Among the findings, 66.7 per cent said they did not maintain security guards and/or electronic systems to monitor data processing functions, and 67.1 per cent said they did not run security checks on employees with access to the company's computers.

That terrorists are aware of this problem is clear from a Reuters dispatch (December 3, 1978) that said that a previously unknown Italian urban guerrilla group, the Armed Anti-Imperialist Movement, set fire to the main computer in a Ministry of Transport Registration Center in Rome and caused millions of dollars worth of damage. Hundreds of thousands of files and microfilms representing more than 20 million documents were also destroyed.

Another aspect of the problem was described in an article in *Business Week* (March 2, 1979):

> Striking British civil servants have unfurled a carefully selective shutdown of government computers that could establish electronic data processing as the ultimate strike weapon. . . . Two unions called a strike on Feb. 26 that pulled the plug on government computers that handled — among other things — defense movements, coded intergovernmental messages, the collection of value added taxes, and farm subsidies. . . . "We are out to disrupt the processes of government administration," [said the union leader]. . . . "Only 1,300 members went out on strike with their full salaries paid by the unions, while the remaining 99.996% stayed on the job." After Foreign Secretary Owen made an unfavorable remark about the strike, cipher clerks in the Foreign Office walked out, shutting down communications with embassies around the world. Said the PCSA's Graham: "Perhaps Dr. Owen will wish he had been a bit more polite when talking to our pickets.

In 1978 the prestigious Foreign Affairs Research Institute of London published a major report on the problem by

Dominic Baron. It described how to cripple a modern industrialized state by a terrorist attack on its computer systems. It would mean the inability to monitor enemy missiles, aircraft, and warships, mobilize reserve forces, and the paralysis of transport and communications. The more subtle threat, he said, derives from the availability of ever cheaper and more sophisticated microprocessors, which the technically expert terrorist group may well use to perfect systems to neutralize elaborate electronic protective devices around sensitive defense installations. Clearly, he emphasized, access to major computing facilities will be open as much to the malefactor as to the good citizen, so it will not be difficult for the "electronic terrorist" to use these facilities to plan optimal strategies for his attacks on the weakest points of some security systems.

The horrific results of a major terrorist crime requiring such high levels of expertise in accessing classified information may nevertheless lead one to forget that such expertise is not qualitatively different from that needed to make unauthorized access to information systems in order to perpetrate fraud, or carry out industrial espionage.

4. The Media Contribution to Mass Destruction

THE average person no doubt considers it difficult to obtain the technological expertise that would be necessary to engage in these terrorist activities. But media insistence upon absolute and unrestrained "freedom of expression" has made the whole thing rather simple. To disabuse the reader of such notions we quote a few titles from a catalog of publications widely advertised and available: *Guide to Germ Warfare, Guide to Chemical and Gas Warfare, Military Explosives, Demolition Materials, Grenades and Pyrotechnics, Boobytraps* ("a treasure-trove of information . . . in 180 information-packed pages with 150 detailed illustrations"), *Land Mine Warfare, British Army Sniper Manual, Explosive Trains, Silencers, Snipers and Assassins, How to Kill* ("probably the most terrifying and gruesome book ever printed"), *Locksmithing and Security Manuals, OSS Special Weapons Catalog,* and *The Plumber's Kitchen: the Secret Story of American Spy Weapons* ("included are full data on the weapons themselves, original photos, specifications"), and on, and on, and on. This list represents but one publisher!

In a February 28, 1976, article entitled "The New American Way of Terrorism" *Newsday* stated that "most libraries have books on the subject — the most popular being *The Anarchist Cookbook* by William Porter. In it are sections on how to make nitroglycerin, mercury fulminate, blasting gelatin, and TNT. "I hate that book," said one bomb expert, "everything is right there. It makes it too easy." One terrorist testified at his trial that he had bought dynamite for his bomb in a casual barroom meeting with a "Mafia-type" character and assembled it from directions in *The Anarchist Cook Book*. He said he was in a bar in Yorkville (New York City) drinking beer when a man at a nearby table remarked that he looked like a revolutionary. He replied: "Yes. And you look like the Mafia. You must sell illegal stuff." When the man nodded yes, they went to the men's room, where the transaction for the dynamite was completed for $200.

A few years ago a new "how-to-do-it" magazine appeared on the newsstands called *Assassin*. The editor claimed to draw on the expertise "of the world's highest paid assassins and some of the key figures in the shadow world of intelligence," none of whom, of course, were identified. It also contained articles on how to build your own nuclear weapon. The editor-publisher, David Kornblum, appealed to the common justification. His purpose, he said, was to shock people into doing something about these "terrible things that are going on."

The film critic of the *Times*, Vincent Canby, was moved to comment on the recent spate of movies on assassinations, among them *Hennessy* and *The Day of the Jackal*. In an article "On Being Entertained by Assassinations" (August 3, 1975), Canby noted that such films are "suggestive." Ought there to be regulation? Ought there to be discussion of limitations on artistic and intellectual freedom to make public persons and the rest of us safer than we are today against the incitements of powerfully made movies? He concluded: "There was . . . the fear that the movie might give ideas to some potential assassin. That probably will always be a problem with films that portray any kind of anti-social behavior whatsoever."

In the March 3, 1976, issue of *TV Guide* FBI Director Clarence Kelley argued, in an article titled "Television is Armed and Dangerous," that TV publicity can produce a chain reaction of crime, especially in airplane hijackings, situations like the SLA-Hearst case, and the ghetto riots of the 1960's. But, as caretaker for a defunct crime-control agency of his own that has felt the power of the media directly, Mr. Kelley dared not presume to suggest anything beyond TV cooperation in providing more balance.

Popular novels also provide the same kind of "entertainment." Frederick Forsyth describes at length in *The Odessa File* how to construct a bomb from materials that can be purchased at any shopping center and attach it to a car. Sam Greenlee describes in *The Spook Who Sat by the Door* (according to UPI, the book was the model for the SLA) the tactics for staging riots and armed insurrections in ghettos. United Artists obligingly made the tactics available to a wider audience with a motion picture publicized as "a shocking screen reality." The cover of the paperback informs us:

Your city is in the sight of a weapon so powerful you can't escape its blast, a weapon loaded with 300 years' worth of hate and hostile neglect. The weapon — a united Black America. This is the story of what could happen when the weapon strikes. . . . It could happen before you finish the book! "An important, original, nitty-gritty book." — Dick Gregory. "Will cause many readers great annoyance — and what more can a writer ask than that?" — Len Deighton.

And then we have *Black Sunday* by Thomas Harris. The terrorist plan here is to rig up a plastic bomb along the lines of a giant claymore mine, attach it to a TV blimp, and then lower it into the Superbowl Stadium at half-time, exploding it in the presence of some 84,000 fans, including the President. This "entertainment" was published one week before the 1975 Superbowl; the movie version opened shortly before the 1976 Superbowl. According to the review in the *Times*, in his book Harris "spares us none of the tricks of successful Doomsday literature. He throws in technology that even Frederick Forsyth would be proud of: the development of the bomb itself, from the smuggling of its plastique into the country in the form of hundreds of dashboard madonnas, to its final testing in miniature (to be certain that the spread of its shrapnel forms a vertical arc of 150 degrees and a horizontal one of 260 degrees — just about right for a stadium crowd)."

In October, 1976, CBS telecast a segment of "Hawaii Five-O" about nuclear terrorism (which was by no means a first for "Hawaii Five-O"). The Atomic Industrial Forum vigorously protested the showing of the program, describing it as "anti-factual and highly emotional." The controversy, curiously, was described not in the entertainment section but in the news columns of the *Times*, which said that "the story involved the theft of plutonium by the band [of terrorists] and the deaths of several persons as a result of the exposure to the chemical element." The spokesman for the Forum said that "exposure to plutonium, if it occurred as described in the story, would not cause death." Another lobbyist for the civilian nuclear power industry was quoted as saying that "the problem we have with the television show is that it makes diversion look ridiculously easy, as if there were no security precautions. It also makes it seem that any high-school kid, with two friends to help him, can build a nuclear bomb." But diversion is ridiculously easy, as we show in this work. And experts in nuclear weapons have demonstrated that three high-school kids could build a nuclear weapon.

The same industry spokesman pointed out also that "a recent made-for-television movie dealt with terrorists taking over a nuclear power plant and that an advance storyline for a forthcoming episode of the ABC series, 'Most Wanted,' gave the plot as 'a large American city threatened with destruction by hijackers of a plutonium convoy.' " He said that even a recent episode of "Mary Hartman, Mary Hartman" introduced a character who was a plutonium terrorist. It was thus clear that by late 1976 TV had discovered the possibility of nuclear terrorism, and was exploiting it to the fullest extent possible. The great danger, of course, is the far greater audience that such shows reach and the ideas they may develop in certain people.

In October, 1976, James Mills (*Report to the Commissioner* and *One Just Man*, the latter about a Kunstler-type lawyer who causes an armed insurrection in New York City by blacks) published his latest "dilly of a thriller," *The Seventh Power*. *Publishers Weekly* described the "novel" as being "about the plausibility of making a homemade nuclear bomb. Two Princeton students put the bomb together. Bobby French is black, the son of a judge. Aizy Tate is a poor little rich girl, an odd-ball, but brilliant at nuclear physics. Stoop, Harlem street black, is the third member of the team. His job: steal the necessary supplies. The evil machine is built. . . . Suspense reaches a nearly unbearable pitch as French, Tate, and Stoop become, in themselves, the world's seventh nuclear power." And, of course, all of Mills's associates in this lucrative literary industry effusively praised the work.

The work was announced with a quarter-page ad in the *Times* laced with highly favorable quotes from Robin Moore, Tom Wolfe, William Stevenson, Richard Condon, and Ira Levin. But ultraliberal Pete Hamill, who reviewed it for the Sunday *Times*, was a bit tremulous and somewhat less enthusiastic about the "novel."

> In the disguise of a taut, skillfully arranged thriller, James Mills has written a very dangerous book.... Mills has written a manual for the construction of an Atomic Bomb. At home. With relatively inexpensive materials, freely available from commercial sources. With plans provided by the United States Government. The inspiration for the novel is clearly John McPhee's 1974 essay-report *The Curve of Binding Energy*, the true story of a physicist named Theodore Taylor, who has been warning against the very real chance that homemade atomic bombs can be easily made and used for purposes of terror. Novelist Mills has recycled journalist McPhee.... [One character] has read McPhee's book (along with Robert Heilbroner's *An Inquiry Into the Human Prospect*). . . . One sentence is underlined twice: "A homemade nuclear bomb is not an impossibility, not even particularly difficult."... All this is told in convincing detail. True, the book as a *novel* suffers as a result; the story swiftly becomes one about a process, rather than about people. . . . The bomb can be used to force the West to feed the starving people of Africa.... The book is more dark prophecy than it is novel.

Hamill, unlike most other reviewers, does stress the enormous danger created by the publication of such works. Evidently they have two purposes — to "entertain" the public and to enrich the author, that is, to make a capitalist out of him. But Hamill appears even more disturbed by literary niceties, such as the question of plagiarism:

> I'm afraid there is more to explore in a review of this book than its author ever intended. A serious literary question must be raised. How much recycling or paraphrasing of someone else's original reporting is permissible to the novelist? This is pertinent because Mills has drawn so extensively on the original reporting of John McPhee. The entire process of building an atomic bomb is presented in a more concise form in McPhee's book, as are some of the scenarios that Mills goes on to dramatize. McPhee tells; Mills shows. McPhee explains; Mills adds a certain amount of flesh to the bones of the explanation.

Hamill then provides a number of examples of the plagiarism he questions. We include here only one:

> McPhee (speculating on his own): "The most densely populated sector of the world is the part of Manhattan Island synecdochically known as Wall Street, where in a third of a square mile, the work-a-day population is half a million people. If all the people were to try to go outdoors at the same time, they could not do so because they are too many for the streets." Mills (through the character of French): "We're taking it to Wall Street, to the Stock Exchange. During work hours there's half a million people there inside a third of a square mile. That's more people than there are in Miami. It's so crowded, if they all came out at the same time, there wouldn't be room on the street for them, they'd have to stand on each other's shoulders." Mills alludes to McPhee's book on several occasions, but I think it's fair to say that *The Seventh Power* would not exist if *The Curve of Binding Energy* had not existed first. . . . The least Mills might do for McPhee is split the money for any movie sale.

Hamill ends by stressing what we have been trying to stress:

As it stands, *The Seventh Power* is certain to reach a larger audience that *The Curve of Binding Energy*, because fiction is a more accessible medium when it is presented as pure entertainment. But the book's very success might make the world more dangerous. . . . Somewhere out there, among the drugstore racks, and in the college paperback shops, in the candystores of a dozen turbulent cities in a very dangerous world, someone might exist who can be seduced down the same path by reading James Mills. That's spooky.

In March, 1979, *The Progressive* submitted an article describing how to fabricate an H-bomb to the Government for clearance. Since *The Progressive* is not the sort of publication that is overly conscientious about submitting its material to the "imperialist" American Government for clearance, it seems obvious that this was a stratagem devised by the "Old Left" journal to "hype" its declining circulation. The ploy succeeded beyond its wildest dreams. The Government went to court to bar publication. *The Progressive* received massive publicity in the media. *The Progressive*'s lawyers contemptuously pointed out in their brief, and quite correctly, that anyone with a library card could get the necessary information. The author had even been given tours of nuclear facilities by officials, and his technical questions were answered in precise detail.

The conflicting values in the case were most appropriately stated by the Federal district judge, Robert W. Warren, in his decision justifying prepublication censorship:

> Stripped to its essence, then, the question before the court is a basic confrontation between the First Amendment right to freedom of the press and national security. . . . [The judge said]: a mistake in ruling against *The Progressive* will seriously infringe cherished First Amendment rights. [However] a mistake in ruling against the United States could pave the way for thermonuclear annihilation for us all. In that event, our right to life is extinguished and the right to publish becomes moot.

5. Playing with LNG: The Times Books Scenario

THE VILLAGE VOICE, a middle-class, left-wing New York City newspaper, published on November 6, 1978, an article by Alexander Cockburn and James Ridgeway under the calculatedly shocking heading: "How To Bring the Nation to Its Knees: The Terror Scenario Jimmy Carter Must Read." The article began:

> Top officials of the U.S. government are now meeting in utmost secrecy to discuss an urgent threat to national security. An astonishing report spells out their concerns.
> Blandly titled "Memorandum for the President on Fuel Systems Vulnerability Within the United States," the report shows that:
> — A single saboteur could paralyze the city of Los Angeles with a hand grenade.
> — The entire city of New York could be held ransom by a terrorist on the bridge of an LNG (Liquefied Natural Gas) tanker.
> — One man gaining entrance to one small room could wreck the oil supply of several states.
> — The nation is as vulnerable to sabotage of its energy lifelines as at any time since the early days of the Second World War. . . .
> This memorandum, of which we have obtained a copy, was prepared by the Inter-Departmental Task Force on Energy.

A note at the end of the article advised the reader: "For a complete version of the report, see *Smoke, Another Jimmy Carter Adventure*, a novel."

The diligent reader, upon obtaining a copy of the novel, or, as it is described on the flyleaf, "the not-so-far-fetched sort-of-novel," discovers that the "report" is a chapter in a work of fiction. There is no source mentioned, no suggestion whatsoever in the novel (short story in length) that the "report" is, as *The Village Voice* had alarmingly stressed, authoritative in nature. The "report" merely appears in typescript, not print, and without any explanation other than its having been obtained from the Government by a fictional character in the previous chapter. (The novel, incidentally, was published by Times Books, a division of *The New York Times*, which purports to be a responsible corporation, unlike those other greedy corporations it periodically excoriates on its editorial pages for being somewhat lacking in social responsibility.)

Of as much significance, however, is that everything published in this "report" is quite true. Of much greater importance is that these rather precise tactics were being published in *The Village Voice*, considering its target audience, and as a novel designed to achieve mass circulation.

The most significant aspects of the "report" are worth quoting at length:

> While the U.S. is abundantly endowed with reserves of major mineral fuels. . . . the supply of these fuels is vulnerable to terrorist attack and interdiction. A survey by this office makes clear that population centers could be severed from fuel supplies with considerable ease. There is presently no federal contingency plan to deal with this threat.
>
> Though it is popularly assumed that terrorists and saboteurs would direct their attention to oil refineries, electric generation equipment, or nuclear power plants, in fact it is beyond doubt that the most vulnerable parts of the energy supply system within the continental U.S. are the transmission facilities for oil, natural gas, and electricity.

Since natural gas and oil are transported mainly through pipelines — some 250,000 miles of them transporting oil alone — the consequent dangers are:

> A gas pipeline can be bombed over a considerable length by a single charge. It will blow up by itself if a break allows air into the line. An air-gas mixture in a pipeline, under right

conditions, can explode and detonate over miles of terrain through cities and industrial centers. Damage to a sizable line would be measured in the millions of dollars and cause complete destruction of segments of the line. It is seldom that just a small section of the line is destroyed. The writer observed an eight-inch spiral weld line that unwound and came out of its ditch for a distance of eight miles. A larger line would result in a worse situation. (M. Stephens, "Vulnerability of Total Petroleum Systems," May, 1973, U.S. Dept. of Interior, Office of Oil and Gas, unclassified.)

The "report" stressed that natural gas pipelines are especially vulnerable to sabotage. Of some 65 pipelines, only 24 carry 97 per cent of the gas, which in turn is more than one third of the nation's total energy supply. Furthermore, only four pipelines are used to carry it from the rich fields of the South and Southwest to metropolitan areas such as New York and Los Angeles. The "report" dourly observes:

Interdiction of the pipeline system would be a simple task for any terrorist group. It can safely be said that any saboteur furnished with the most rudimentary equipment (a shovel, a bulldozer) could disrupt the integrity of a pipeline.

Maps of pipelines are available from the Department of Energy and are routinely published in industry journals.

The "report" stresses, as we also have emphasized several times, that because the United States is so technologically sophisticated, it is unusually vulnerable to sabotage. Many compressor stations, for example, are controlled automatically and are completely unmanned. Repair crews are quite scarce. And in the older cities along the Eastern Seaboard the gas pipes are old and dilapidated. If terrorists sharply increased the gas pressure in lines serving residences and public buildings by merely turning a dial, the lines could rupture and cause fires throughout the city.

"Scenario No. 1" in the "report" described how to take Los Angeles off-line. Having first obtained a map from the Department of Energy or an industry trade journal and located the target, the lines could be easily dug out with shovels or a bulldozer and then blown up. Recovery would take several days, and industries and consumers would be without energy in the interim.

And although oil is much less volatile than natural gas, it nonetheless offers many interesting possibilities for terrorists.

One small room, in a large southern city, houses the complete pipeline control system and controls oil movement over several states. Valves can be closed or opened, pumps can be started or stopped, even though they are miles away. Forced entry to the computerized center, the cutting of wires, the mutilation of the printed circuit boards, the burning out of low voltage circuits by tying them to the house current, the careless use of a strong magnet, could suddenly put the entire system back on hand operation. Each control valve, of many hundreds, would have to be visited, but now only a few men are available to run the system. There are no repair crews except for contractors in most cases.

Electrical supply systems are also quite vulnerable. The "report" criticizes the utilities, especially those on the East Coast, for having failed to develop an interconnecting grid system. After discussing the 1977 New York blackout, it concludes: "It is the judgment of the Task Force that the Eastern Seaboard is vulnerable to attack and grave destruction at every point from Washington to the Canadian border." (In February, 1979, *The New York Times* published a lengthy background story with precise details and two large maps pinpointing every power station and transmission line of the Northeast Power Coordinating Council. It contained all the information any terrorist could possibly desire. At the same time, Arthur

Hailey's *Overload*, which contains precise details as to how to engage in terrorism against a power company, was number one on the *Times*'s best-seller list.)

Communications and computers, according to the "report," can easily be sabotaged by terrorists.

Since computers play such an important role in the management of energy fuel transmission systems, it is important to realize that computer control centers are especially vulnerable. The possibility of forced entry by a group of competent saboteurs is an obvious danger, and one where protective measures can be taken. But there arc far more subtle forms of sabotage. For example, a saboteur may pose as an employee, gain entrance to the computer operations, and man a position for months or years. Through artifice, he can wreck the computer and bring down the energy system. He may adopt any one of a number of tried techniques. The "Trojan Horse" trick is one example. It involves the saboteur twisting the program in such a way that all control is given to one terminal of which he has command. The "time bomb" trick involves the saboteur programming some seemingly harmless word, such as the name of the saboteur, in such a way that once his name is printed out, all the computer tapes are erased. It is, of course, known that a computer can be severely damaged through the use of magnets or by the simple pouring of a carbonated drink over the works.

The "report" expresses particular concern over the problem of Liquefied Natural Gas. One misplaced, or well-placed, stroke of a match, it warns, could turn "the lower end of Manhattan into a firestorm." It envisions the following scenario:

Terrorists fire a projectile at an LNG tanker as it proceeds through a populous port. The ship would explode or let off an inflammable gas cloud over population centers nearby. While the Coast Guard supplies protection for LNG tankers, it would be impossible to stop an attack of this kind.

The passage of many LNG tankers through U.S. waters brings them close to the landing and takeoff runways of major airports. Boston is a prime example. Given terrorist takeover of an LNG tanker, airport operation could be severely impaired. Worse, the release of the invisible gas at the end of a runway would, if it enveloped an adjacent aircraft, detonate in a catastrophic ball of fire.

A group of terrorists approach, board and take command of an LNG tanker, threatening to blow it up in the port of a city such as New York, Boston, Philadelphia, or Los Angeles, unless certain demands are met.

Assuming the takeover was close to shore, there is no military means of recovery which would not gravely imperil many hundreds of lives and extensive property. It should be pointed out that since there are no workable evacuation plans for any city in the U.S., it would be impossible to secure the inhabitants in the event of such a threat.

If, on the other hand, the terrorists were foolish enough to commandeer an LNG tanker at sea, the ship could be blown up by plane or submarine. Although the crew would, of course, be lost along with the terrorists, it is of interest to note that many LNG tankers are foreign flag vessels manned by crews of other nations. The Department of Defense and State Department should comment on reaction by other nations to military attack.

A few weeks after Times Books published this "report," many of the nation's newspapers carried (December, 1978) a photo of a French supertanker (LNG), *Mostafa Ben Boulaid*, 914 feet long and carrying 31.5 million gallons of LNG, entering Boston Harbor. The caption noted that the ship was so large that it seemed to dwarf the Boston skyline and that critics had pointed out that an accident would have meant total disaster for the City of Boston. And this tanker was one of the smaller LNG carriers. The ship made its entry to the totally cleared harbor at high tide to clear the channel, but that caused it to pass under a harbor bridge with only fifteen feet to spare.

All that would have been required, for example, would be for a terrorist to have planted a timed explosive on that bridge, or merely to have dropped something from a helicopter or small plane, and Boston would have been totally wiped out. That tanker alone is expected to stop fourteen to seventeen times a year at Boston.

Approximately 40 per cent (according to most sources) of this nation's energy needs is supplied by natural gas. But in order to import gas economically, it must be liquefied, reduced to 1/600th of its vapor volume. The basic problem is that it will not liquefy until it is − 260°F., making it nearly impossible to contain. It is thus loaded in giant "thermos bottles," twelve stories high, in enormous tankers. When (not *if*, the experts maintain) it is released into the atmosphere, the − 260°F. gas, coming into contact with an ambient temperature of approximately 60°, will result in violent boiling, shattering anything it comes in contact with, including the ship transporting it. If a ship entering a harbor had a routine collision or grounding, ran a bridge abutment, were rammed, had a fire or explosion (all routine accidents for tankers), it would rupture the "thermos bottle." The LNG, as it flows out, would boil, reverting back to its natural vapor state, and expand to 600 times its volume in its containerized state. It would successively asphyxiate, flash-freeze, and french-fry everything in its path. Since the vapors are heavier than air, they do not flow up and away from the ground, but down to it, going into sewers and drainpipes. The vapor cloud becomes windborne and flows, searching for a source of ignition. Ultimately reaching one, it will cause a flashback, i.e., the incineration will race to the source of the gas, which is a vast storage tank, and/or adjacent ship, resulting in detonation, explosion, deflagration. The real root of the LNG problem is that these huge storage tanks and receiving facilities for the ships are located within dense population zones, surrounded by heavy industry,

fuel storage tank farms, petrochemical plants, and refineries, so that the release of the gas into the atmosphere
would result in an enormous domino effect. There are now
two such storage facilities within New York City, one
quite close to midtown Manhattan and the other quite
close to the heavily congested downtown financial district.
By mid-1978 there were 187 facilities in operation in the
nation, and the industry was just in its infancy.

One sentence from the GAO report of 1978 on Liquefied
Energy Gases Safety gives some indication of what might
result from an accident or terrorism: "The closest analogy
to an accident in one of the facilities would be a major
bombing raid in World War II." The total energy of bombs
dropped in the 1945 raid on Tokyo — which killed 83,000
— is 1 per cent of the energy in one large LNG tank.

The rather small TETCO tank on Staten Island that
blew up and killed over forty workers was empty. There
had been a small protest the day before, and TETCO had
condemned it as hysterical. It had also been certified as
gas free by marine chemists, and been purged with inert
gas for ten months.

A small, poorly funded neighborhood group, BLAST
(Bring Legal Action to Stop the Tanks), has kept this $120
million facility empty for five years, costing the company
$650,000 a month in maintenance fees alone. The original
company has since gone bankrupt, and the tank has been
taken over by Public Service Gas and Electric of New
Jersey. There have been Congressional hearings for five
years to decide what to do with it, to fill it or not. If not,
then what do you do with it?

One problem is that since such facilities usually require
over a hundred different permits, no one Government
body is ultimately responsible.

In 1978 a short work on the hazards of LNG was published for the mass market. Entitled *Time Bomb, LNG*:
The Truth about Our Newest and Most Dangerous Energy

Source, it was written by Peter van der Linde, with Naomi A. Hintze. The author is a captain in the U.S. Merchant Marine and has frequently commanded (oil) supertankers.

Van der Linde pointed out that safety precautions are commonly ignored on tankers, and that tanker accidents are escalating, not decreasing. (The Coast Guard also reported in December, 1978, that tanker losses are increasing.) When you work with something for a while, van der Linde observed, you become complacent. For example, in the Staten Island facility they were required, among many other precautions, to use no-spark type clothing, and not carry or use cigarette lighters. They found, after the explosion, not only cigarette lighters, but a revolver and inflammable after-shave lotion.

Van der Linde pertinently asks that if there are 40,000 oil spills *reported* to the Coast Guard in this nation alone, why may we not expect at least one LNG spill? We lose, he says, an average of one merchant ship a day. There are collisions every hour of every day. Why should we believe that this will not happen to an LNG ship? Accidents are inevitable. Nothing is totally fail-safe. Such ships, unprotected, located in dense population zones, he warns, are perfect targets for terrorists, saboteurs, or hijackers. Storage tanks should be relocated, he argues cogently, to more remote areas. But since that would be expensive for the company, it is unlikely to happen. Gloomily, he concludes that there will probably not be even a minimal effort at solution before there is some horrible disaster. The gas companies, he emphasizes, are *not* lawbreakers. They are being allowed to do it. On the TV program "Sixty Minutes" Mike Wallace indignantly demanded of John Cabot (Cabot Industries) in Boston: "Don't you have any moral responsibility, any moral fibre at all?" Cabot replied that "when you change the laws, we'll abide by them. But until such time as you do, we're going ahead with it."

Fire-fighting systems, van der Linde sardonically observes, are mere public relations window-dressing when it
comes to LNG. The superpumpers in all LNG plants are of
no use. No one can say that water will even begin to fight
an LNG fire. Chemicals, which are also emphasized in
corporate safety reports, have been without much success
in fighting even Liquefied Propane Gas (LPG) fires, which
are substantially less volatile. No fire-fighting material
known to man will work in an LNG fire. New York City
Fire Department orders consist of one word: evacuation. If
possible later, when the fire dies down, the Fire Department will search and rescue. Winds will be in excess of
1,000 mph and temperature in excess of 3,000°F. in the
center of the kill zone. LNG will even cause a flameless
explosion when liquid hits liquid, that is, when LNG spills
from the ship and hits the river.

In a fifteen-volume California State report prepared
under Governor Brown, industry admits that 100,000 will
die in Los Angeles if the facility on (the appropriately
named) Terminal Island goes, which is built half on a
landfill and half on the San Andreas fault. Industry, van
der Linde stresses, isn't arguing that the consequences
will not be catastrophic if an accident occurs. It agrees.
But its spokesmen contend they have a zero-defect free
system, something which is regarded as impossible in any
other industry or human endeavor. In *Time Bomb* van der
Linde proves the contrary. A more realistic estimate for
California by Government officials and other experts, he
says, is a million or more deaths. (With the panic casualties, it would be far higher.) For van der Linde this is not a
reasonable risk for a reasonable return.

Affordable realistic alternatives are available. One is
offshore sea islands, floating or stationary. The United
States is well suited for creating such islands because of
the shallow continental shelf. In the event of an accident
fewer would die. If it were an environmental issue, such as

dead birds, well-financed groups like the Sierra Club would exert enormous pressure. But here only people are involved.

In van der Linde's *Time Bomb* scenario an LNG ship is rammed at the dock and New York City is leveled. Millions are killed. The scenario is perfectly plausible, the author points out, according to many scientists and marine experts in various fields. He "quadruple-sourced" *Time Bomb*, he says, in expectation of industry attacks, and it was now "being gone over with a magnifying glass by industry sources." But most of the research upon which he relied was done by company employees, he explains, since these are the main sources available. And that information is obviously stacked in favor of the industry. Even so, it is horrifying.

In contrast to van der Linde and "Sixty Minutes," the *Christian Science Monitor* (November 30, 1977) under the headline "LNG: A Ticking Time Bomb?" described the docking regulations at Boston Harbor as strict. The Coast Guard, it said, must meet LNG tankers four miles out and escort them in. All other ships must keep out of the area.

Yet the Congressional Office of Technology Assessment (OTA) report, issued two months earlier, had concluded that "the present method of operation may be very costly and unworkable as increasing numbers of LNG tankers enter service." It stressed that new safety standards would have to be considered as the tankers became larger and more complex. By 1985, it was estimated, 175 LNG tankers would be in use. The report stressed also that existing fire-fighting methods could not extinguish an LNG fire on water: "It is generally agreed that, if the vapor from a large liquefied natural gas spill ignites, it would be beyond the capability of exisiting fire-fighting methods to extinguish it.... Therefore, the key to reducing the hazard of a liquefied natural gas fire is a strong prevention program."

On February 22, 1978, *The New York Times* published material from a 515-page draft report of the GAO, not yet made public. The GAO said that both LNG and LPG facilities were subject to "catastrophic failure" and that Federal licensing procedures were "clearly inadequate to protect the public health and safety." The *Times* noted that the unreleased draft report had already brought forth a vigorous wave of protests from the gas and utilities industries. It reported that the head of the GAO's Energy and Minerals Division had testified before the House Commerce Committee's Subcommittee on Energy and Power that security procedures and physical barriers intended to protect liquefied natural gas and liquefied petroleum gas facilities "are generally not adequate to deter even an untrained amateur saboteur." One major reason for such a lack of security is that "present corporate structures and legal limits on liability protect the parent corporation and diminish incentives for safety." As for LPG facilities, he concluded it was highly likely that at least some of them would be hit during their lifetimes by floods, storms, or earthquakes more powerful than they were designed to withstand. In contrast, "even though nuclear plants are located in nonurban areas, they are built to much higher standards than LNG facilities in urban areas because of the perceived potential for causing off-site damage."

Although two chapters in the GAO report conclude that facilities outside urban areas were large enough to carry the load now being handled by urban facilities, a spokesman for Con Ed in New York City said that its LNG facility in Astoria, Queens, which can hold the equivalent of a billion cubic feet of gas, was 90 per cent full, and a spokesman for Brooklyn Union Gas said its facilities in Greenpoint hold the equivalent of 1.6 billion cubic feet of natural gas.

By this time, and rather belatedly, Federal and New York City officials were becoming concerned about the storage in, and shipment through, New York of highly volatile substances. In a lengthy backgrounder on page one, the *Times* reminded its readers of some previous near misses. (It should be noted that industry officials regard near misses, since they are "only" near, as proof that their fail-safe systems are working perfectly.) To cite just one instance of a near miss!

On June 4, 1976, a railroad tank car carrying 32,000 gallons of LPG derailed in the Bronx. During an attempt to right it, it was accidentally dropped two feet. Although the pressurized car did not explode, a similar car did the previous February in Tennessee, killing twelve persons. The Bronx accident caused grave concern in the New York City Fire Department, especially since it was the third derailment since the mid 1960's of a car carrying liquefied gas. In a letter to the Federal Government, the Fire Department warned that such accidents have the potential of making "a major disaster."

Because of the tangled legal maze surrounding the movement and storage of such highly combustible liquefied gases, the Fire Department is unable to halt such shipments through New York City. Industry officials insisted, as usual, and very much in contrast to the GAO report, that "elaborate safety precautions are taken." But the *Times* went on to point out that the Fire Department, the GAO, and the Department of Transporation (DOT), as well as a number of well-known scientists, expressed serious reservations about the storage and transportation of liquefied fuels near areas where large numbers of people live and work. The Federal Railroad Administration replied to the Fire Department with a single form letter, and LPG cars continued to roll over the deteriorating rail beds in New York City. In fact, the *Times* reported, none of the

Federal agencies involved seem to have any idea of just how much of this material is moving through New York City. The American Trucking Associations estimated over 1,000 trucks probably were involved in New York City. DOT reported there were 1,146 hazardous materials accidents involving trucks in 1975, and between 1971 and 1976 there was an average of 129 railroad accidents per year involving hazardous materials. During the extremely cold winter of 1977 the Fire Department permitted Brooklyn Union Gas to transport 25 truckloads of LNG across the Verrazano Bridge. Industry officials were insisting that if an accident occurred at a storage facility, it would cause no harm to the public. Dr. Edward Teller and other prominent scientists vehemently disputed such contentions. The *Times* again referred to the still unreleased GAO draft report, which, it said, concluded that a serious storm, an earthquake, or terrorist attack could cause a major rupture in installations used to store LNG in more than a hundred locations in the United States and could result in the deaths of tens of thousands. The GAO emphatically criticized the Federal Government for its lack of response to the extreme danger.

At about this time Indians and the Marine Corps on the West Coast were fighting the plan to locate a major LNG terminal in California. While the Indians, 25 Chumash, upset about the "desecration of our sacred.land," were successful in causing the State Coastal Commission to change the site from nearby Santa Barbara to Point Conception, the Marine Corps became rather upset, with somewhat more justification. The promoters of the terminal (Western LNG Associates, a partnership of PG&E and Pacific Lighting Company) were insisting that the site be located at Point Conception because it would save them money.

That site happens to be located on the San Andreas fault. The State Commission, seeking to avoid that problem, suggested Camp Pendleton. The Marine Corps maintained that it woud constitute a grave danger to the 30,000 personnel on the base and the adjoining city of Oceanside. The commanding general cited the constant risk of damage to the pipeline from heavy military vehicles and unexploded ammunition. He said that low-level attack aircraft, carrying 500-lb. bombs, would have to be rerouted. One of the greatest hazards, in the opinion of Marine and Congressional leaders, is that it is only five miles south of the San Onofre nuclear power station, built on Marine beachfront by a special act of Congress in 1964. An accident at either facility could trigger a double disaster *(New York Times,* May 21, 1978).

In late July, 1978, the final version of the GAO report was released to Congress. It comprised three volumes, 1,000 pages. It was immediately attacked by the American Gas Association as being inordinately concerned with terrorism and "unreal hypothetical situations." The Departments of Commerce and Transportation (lobbying for their respective corporate interests) also attacked the report. DOT opposed, for example, any ban on LNG trucks or rail cars passing through populated areas. The GAO warned that sabotage dangers are high and that readily available weapons could be used to release dangerous gas clouds from tank trucks and rail tankers. It said that the contents of a single gas truck could fill a hundred miles of 6-foot diameter sewer or 15 miles of subway. It also said that many gas storage tanks had only a small earthquake safety margin, and that that margin was almost certain to be exceeded somewhere in the next fifty years.

Tacked onto the end of this story in the *Times* was a paragraph stating that the LNG terminal for Point Conception (on the San Andreas fault) had been approved by California's Public Utilities Commission. The decision overrode the State Coastal Commission's decision to locate it in Camp Pendleton.

Meanwhile, the Firemen's Training Center of Nassau County, New York, conducted an explosion of liquefied propane, which is trivial in comparison to LNG or even LPG. It was, according to *Newsday*, frightening. The tank held only a hundred pounds, nothing in comparison to what we have been discussing. Nonetheless, the spent cylinder traveled over a six-story building. What the Fire Department was interested in was safety in regard to something as tiny as outdoor grills. The town of Hempstead used the demonstration to announce it was preparing what would be the first local laws in the county to regulate the sale and use of liquefied propane. The fuel is widely available throughout the nation and could easily be used to set off LNG or LPG.

At the same time, corporate and labor interests continued to lobby for their cause with articles such as the one in *Forbes* (September 18, 1978) entitled "A Funny Thing Happened on the Way to LNG." The gist of the article was evident from its subheading: "Is America becoming the red-tape capital of the world? Consider the antics in California over the import of liquefied natural gas." Terrorism, accidents, or building terminals on the San Andreas fault were not mentioned. Panhandle, Eastern, and other corporate giants continued to use full-page ads in business and news magazines to herald the advent of huge cryogenic tankers as the solution to America's energy needs.

Some indication of what might happen can be gleaned from the pipline blast in Mexico (November 3, 1978). It should be stressed that this was natural gas in gas form, not liquefied, which is 600 times more concentrated and much more volatile in various ways. But even a blast like this could be done in a populated area and with far greater casualties. This blast occurred in the jungles. A huge fireball killed more than fifty persons and left a deep crater where the workers' camp had been. According to one witness, "It shook the whole area. I could see parts of human bodies, trees, animals, houses and cars flying through the air." The company statement said that the blast was caused by a leak from "faulty material," but did not elaborate.

Concurrently oil and gas industry executives were, according to the *Washington Post,* in late 1978 urging customers to switch to natural gas because of a natural gas glut. And if they are building all these tankers, we can be sure they are going to use them, since they are enormously expensive.

The American Gas Association had taken the unusual step of calling a press conference in January, 1978, to denounce the report when it was in the drafting stage (thus a leak). While officials of gas companies argued that the report was inordinately concerned with sabotage, the GAO noted that the "petroleum companies in this country have been the targets of sabotage."

Jack Anderson also wrote several columns on the problem. In one he stated: "We've reported previously that existing regulations render many American cities almost helpless against the threat of a fiery inferno. A confidential staff memo to Representative John Dingell (D. Mich.) describes the industry's lobbying as 'virulent if somewhat inept.'" Well, virulent, yes, but hardly inept. He too referred to the GAO warnings. Some of the pipeline used to transport natural gas was installed before the Civil War.

The above-cited fictional "Memorandum for the President on Fuel Systems Vulnerability Within the United States" concluded with a number of recommendations:

> An executive order of the president requiring that all public and private electric utilities establish a national grid, and a similar order for natural gas pipelines.

But for LNG it depressingly concluded: "It is impossible to demonstrate adequate safety procedures and calls for military escorts for LNG tankers within U.S. territorial waters."

Its overall conclusion was:

It is clear from the foregoing survey that despite procedures recommended above, the United States Government cannot secure the nation against fuel vulnerability. Though increased alertness in guarding energy systems must be implemented, it is clear that the most effective security will be preemptive: a stepped-up program of intelligence and surveillance of all potential saboteur and terrorist groups; a computer bank of all such individuals and groups; ongoing penetration of their organizations and advance intelligence on their intentions.

The Village Voice article, resuming its role as "deceit's own child," as dutiful public interest reporter, then predicted that that conclusion was "bound to cause a storm among civil libertarians."

But whether the authors were merely pixieish, pixilated, or agents provocateurs, ironically they are quite correct, indeed prescient. Yet such precautions need not arouse a storm of protest. They and others are the instruments of Crisis Government, and have been seen by most major democratic political philosphers and very many prominent liberal academics as a necessary aspect of any democratic system in time of grave crisis.

PART III

Crisis Government

1. Where We Are

IF THE major nations of the world, led by the United States and the Soviet Union, were to give up their strategic weapons arsenals and put an end to their organized capacities to produce replacement arms, would that mark the end of the "age of nuclear terror" that began in the closing months of World War II?

Back in the spring of 1978, at the time of the murder of Italy's former President Aldo Moro by terrorists of the Italian Red Brigades, James Reston of *The New York Times* morosely contemplated the problem of technological terrorism and concluded that the Moro killing was a "startling reminder of the fragility of all civilized nations." The trouble with civilized nations, he lamented, is that they persist in "worrying these days about classic wars in invasion across national borders, and they debate endlessly over cruise missiles, backfire bombers, and neutron artillery shells that can kill fleets of tanks." Yet there are obviously other kinds of warfare to worry about in our time, particulary the kinds involving technological terror, which "desperate minorities" are now increasingly capable of unleashing. In Reston's words:

> We are probably not at the end but at the beginning of this tyranny of militant minorities. The more people crowd into the cities of the world, the more vulnerable cities become to the sabotage of desperate political organizations like the Red Brigades.

For example, any terrorist group, no matter how small, that knows what manholes to go down to get at the electrical guts or switches of any major city, can terrorize the life of that city. And as we move into the age of nuclear electric power, as we are bound to do as petroleum supplies run out, the problem of sabotage is likely to become more serious. . . . If they can control a nuclear energy plant, or even a railroad train carrying nuclear wastes, they can hold whole cities and countries for ransom. In that event, they can threaten to dump nuclear wastes into the harbor of Stockholm or the rivers of Germany and pollute them for generations. This is not a crazy speculation: it is a practical possibility every country dealing with modern terrorists is now having to face.

A few months before, in November, 1977, Robert H. Kupperman, head of President Carter's Cabinet Committee to Combat Terrorism, had very vividly suggested how very close we had already come to the "practical possibility" Reston refers to. In his report to the committee he headed Kupperman had warned that terrorists might indeed soon be able to paralyze entire cities in the United States, and he had urged on that account that a Federal crisis management group be set up to deal with such potential catastrophes. Outlining the scope of the potential threat, he described what we could expect would happen if a New York City power failure like that of July, 1977, lasted five days instead of two:

> Looters would run wild, fires starting at random, and jittery National Guardsmen shooting into crowds of panicked people. Food and water would become scarce, the sanitation system would collapse, and the rats, which outnumber the people, would be close to achieving a permanent victory. The point is that "nature," with the aid of human inefficiency, produced the two-day siege, but a trained, quite small paramilitary force could take the City of New York — or any large metropolitan area — off-line for extended periods of time.

Why hadn't some terrorist band seized the occasion of the 1977 blackout to put New York City off-line? Why haven't the mounting opportunities for technological terrorism that our society now offers been more effectively "explored" by terrorists? Up until August, 1978, one of the most widely accepted answers to such questions was surely that of Walter Laqueur. Through his many-faceted activities as a professor at the University of Tel Aviv and at Georgetown's Center for Strategic and International Studies, as director of the Institute of Contemporary History and Wiener Library in London, and, more particularly, on the strength of his books *Guerrilla* and *Terrorism*, Laqueur has long distinguished himself as surely the most widely quoted "authority" on the subject. In his major books and in many articles, at least until August, 1978, he regularly dismissed the likelihood of technological terrorism; and it would be difficult to overestimate the harm his insistence on that view has already caused, and is likely to cause in future, despite his apparent reversal of it in 1978.

We get a fair suggestion of the character and measure of Laqueur's influence in this regard in an otherwise insightful article by Drew Middleton *(The New York Times,* November 13, 1977), which described terrorism as a new type of warfare destined to be used increasingly by governments rather than by terrorist bands. Relying primarily on two CIA reports and on Laqueur's *Terrorism* and Brian Jenkins's *International Terrorism,* Middleton wrote:

> Every source consulted on the subject, official and unofficial, emphasized the danger of terrorists acquiring weapons of mass destruction. The CIA reported that "individual terrorist groups already have the capacity of manufacturing or otherwise acquiring a variety of weapons or agents of mass destruction," and that "more will be in a position to exercise this option in the future." But two reasons were advanced why terrorists might decline to do so: the risk of violently adverse public reaction and the assumption that "terrorists are in business to influence people, not to exterminate them." Mr. Laqueur's book notes that the invention of dynamite in 1866 was hailed by the anarchist of those days as the ultimate weapon, "a panacea for the solution of all political and social problems." The possibility of a terrorist group's acquiring nuclear materials is taken extremely seriously by law enforcement agencies. But the obstacles to any theft of any such materials or their development into an actual weapon are formidable, as Mr. Laqueur emphasizes. The probability is low, he says, that terrorists would have the skills, resources or opportunities to convert nuclear materials into weapons. Besides stealing the raw nuclear fuel itself, for instance, they would have to acquire the extremely bulky facilities to enrich it to weapons grade. "The popular idea of a nuclear device produced in a garage and transported on a tricycle seems to belong for the time being to the realm of fantasy," Mr. Laqueur wrote, explaining that the weight of such a device would be at least one ton and perhaps two.

It was Laqueur's contention all along that, while the *potential* for effective use of modern means of mass destruction was great, it would be a long time before the potential could so much as begin to be actualized. In October, 1977, following the West German raid on a hijacked Lufthansa plane at Mogadishu, Somalia, *Time* published a lengthy cover story on terrorism, relying heavily on Laqueur and quoting him finally to the effect that, "in ten or fifteen years, terrorists will have the weapons of superviolence; then perhaps even a single person will be able to blackmail an entire town, district or country." On the assumption that we still have ten or fifteen years to prepare ourselves, the *Time* writers admonished on their own: "To combat tomorrow's terrorist, new and creative measures, as well as an unprecedented degree of international cooperation, will be required. The one certainty is that civilization's war on terrorism will go on."

Even as late as August, 1978, Laqueur's estimate of the time it would take for terrorists to catch up with the opportunities our age offers them was being echoed in State Department publications like *GIST* (officially characterized as "a quick reference aid in U.S. foreign relations primarily for Government use"). In the August issue we read: "Technological advances afford the terrorist many new opportunities:

An instant worldwide audience. The development of satellite communications to facilitate media coverage has been invaluable to the terrorist who relies on attracting public attention to his cause.

New types of weapons. The terrorist arsenal now includes many types of automatic weapons and conventional explosives. Additionally, terrorist use of man-portable anti-tank and/or anti-aircraft weapons cannot be ruled out.

And it continued in virtually the same words as Laqueur:

> Although terrorists could obtain the materials and tech-
> nology to improvise a nuclear device, this is a difficult and
> dangerous task. Moreover, the threat of infliction of mass
> casualties would probably harm rather than help the ter-
> rorists' political cause.

But just about a month before those words appeared in
GIST Laqueur had completely reversed himself on this
score in an interview published in the July 22, 1978, issue
of *U.S. News and World Report*. Previously he had been
quite convinced, as we have seen, that for valid
revolutionary political reasons terrorists would not avail
themselves of the options of mass destruction. But now, in
response to the most important questions posed to him, he
did not hesitate to answer:

> Today's terrorism has become indiscriminate — far more
> brutal than in the past. . . . I am less optimistic about the
> future. I see some potentially grave dangers ahead. There is a
> possibility of terrorists getting hold of weapons of what is
> technically called "superviolence" — not only nuclear but
> biological and chemical weapons as well. With these weapons
> of superviolence, one perhaps can destroy a whole country.
> Admittedly this is illogical, irrational, because the terrorists
> would destroy not only their enemies but their friends and
> even their families. The problem is that terrorists frequently
> are not rational people. . . . A decision was made by rev-
> olutionaries to transform the struggle from guerrilla warfare
> in the countryside to terrorism in the cities. . . . When the
> revolutionaries were operating in the countryside, they could
> kill a dozen soldiers in an ambush, and there was not mention
> of it in the press. By contrast, they found that a relatively
> minor terrorist incident staged in a city would be covered by
> American television and *The New York Times*.

"We're Paving the Way for a Real 'Black Sunday' " was
the title of *Newsday*'s Bob Wiemer column of July 23,

1978. After quoting Walter Laqueur's *U.S. News & World Report* interview, in which Laqueur had reversed his previous emphatic statements and now with as much emphasis pointed out the grave dangers likely from technological terrorism, Wiemer also quoted the LEAA (Law Enforcement Assistance Administration) report of March 2, 1977, "that if a single ounce of anthrax were introduced into the air-conditioning system of a domed stadium, the 70,000 or 80,000 folks present could be infected within an hour, and that any terrorist group with reasonable resources and talent should be able to make an atomic weapon with about half the power of the Hiroshima bomb."

Wiemer was, however, even more appalled at the lack of coverage the report received. "It drew," he stressed, "far less attention than it deserved, perhaps because it said things neither the incumbent administration nor many liberal editors wanted to hear." Citing the report's conclusion that the decline of radical activity in the United States in recent years is a false calm, that we must see in the current social situation an accumulation of trouble for the future, and that there will surely come a time when once again socioeconomic conditions will generate violent reactions, he was amazed that the report was mentioned only once in the volume of the *Readers' Guide* covering the period in which it was issued: "It was ignored. Instead of increasing its scrutiny of potential terrorists and their organizations, the Justice Department turned to the task of demoralizing the FBI."

Wiemer is quite correct. *The New York Times* continues to push for an even greater destabilization of our intelligence agencies. After briefly reviewing past wiretaps and related actions by the FBI, it declared editorially, and ironically, on December 7, 1978: "The only lasting security lies in new laws to govern the activities of the law enforcement and intelligence agencies." But, as Wiemer observes, "these idiocies do not mean the danger is receding. More likely it's mounting faster than ever." He concludes with a quotation from Robert Kupperman: "We're well trained to deal with yesterday's terrorism. We urgently need a plan to deal with tomorrow's."

In the lengthy National Advisory Commission report of March 2, 1977, the panel of experts warned that the condition of many large cities "is more desperate than it was during the most serious riots of the 1960s." They felt that a renewal of urban disorder is quite possible, as well as prison rioting, an increase of incidents of hostage-taking, and conventional terrorism. But they stressed especially the threat from new high technology weapons.

To deal with such problems of mass violence they recommended legislation that would permit disruption of the activities of suspected groups and other unusually tough measures. One of its main recommendations was that law-enforcement agencies be given specific power to gather intelligence on individuals and groups that "might become involved" in violence or civil disorder. If a terrorist group were inclined to fabricate nuclear, bacteriological, or chemical weapons, as of now officials would not know about it until it was too late. The gathering of such intelligence and the maintenance of computerized files on suspects or possibles has become almost nonexistent since Watergate and the investigations of, and attacks on, the CIA and FBI. But the panel concluded that it is "unquestionably necessary" that law-enforcement agencies be given the power, under specific legislation, to carry out covert activity "designed to combat the activities, the organization or the existence of those against whom they are directed."

The danger of terrorists using high technology weapons of mass destruction, it concluded, is so great that every state should have the power to pass emergency legislation quickly. Police power under emergency powers should include "the power of search without warrant of persons and property," the power to "enter premises by force and without warrant," and the right to detain people without arresting them. It further stressed that law-enforcement personnel who happen to exceed their emergency powers should not be held personally liable, either criminally or civilly, for any harm stemming from their behavior. The relative quiet of the past several months, it warned, "is a false calm, and we must see in the current social situation an accumulation of trouble for the future."

Although he had not originally ordered it, James Earl Carter was the President who received the National Advisory Commission's report. On March 10, 1977 — a few days after the report was released — the matter came up at a Presidential news conference. One reporter, in the guise of asking a question, made a kind of brief and highly loaded speech, in which he challenged the President to say, on the spot, whether he favored "certain recommendations of the commission." Taking the matter completely out of context, as if it were some updated version of the Nixon Reelection Campaign Committee schemes for dealing with White House lawn protestors, the reporter said: "Well, sir, in the report there were certain recommendations, such as the use of mass arrests, the use of preventive detention, some of the very things that were used in the sixties and later ruled inappropriate in the courts, and I wondered, sir, what you felt about this problem involving human rights in the United States."

Had he not been a first-term President seeking his party's nominations for a possible second term, Mr. Carter might have responded differently than he did. He might conceivably have taken his cue from one of our more eminent retired ambassadors and former governors, ably representing the traditions of an old New England family — John David Lodge — who, in a recent letter to *The New York Times*, drew on his long experience in revolutionary trouble spots of Europe and South America to urge that, for its own domestic good, our government should discipline itself to become "more geopolitical and less evangelical" in its conduct of foreign policy. And then, drawing the domestic lesson, he concluded:

> If we could stop preaching, we might even be able to learn something from our friends in Argentina, Uruguay, and Chile regarding how they have successfully handled and are handling the most cunning, cynical, vicious, brutal, relentless challenge of our time. When will we catch on that the ideological conflict is taking place in a jungle world? . . . In Argentina, Chile, Paraguay, Bolivia, and in Brazil they have sought the confrontation out of which victory has gradually emerged. The security forces are prevailing against the imperialistic drive from Moscow via Havana. In the countries of Western Europe, the will to resist, sapped by years of war, has been further eroded by chicanery and by raw terrorism. . . The contrast between the healthy zest for the struggle in South America and the decadent defeatism rampant in Western Europe is dramatic.

Instead of the counsels of tough ex-ambassadors or tough national advisory commissions, what a first-term President seeking reelection is most inclined to heed, it seems, is the advice of election ad-men, who now look upon TV nightly host Johnny Carson as a model of how a first-term President ought to look and talk if he hopes to have an "extended run" hosting the White House show. The rule is: Don't be *heavy*, or the relaxing bedroom audience will "switch off." How did the President feel about the hard-and-heavy recommendations of the National Advisory Commission for equipping ourselves to face the challenge of revolutionary terrorism? Approximating the tone of a successful night show host, Mr. Carter said:

> I would be opposed to mass arrests and I would be opposed to preventive detention as a general policy and even as a specific policy unless it was an extreme case. Obviously, in a 600-page report there would be things with which we would

agree and things with which we would disagree. I've not seen the report. I'm not familiar with it. But I think that the abuses in the past have in many cases exacerbated the disharmonies that brought about demonstrations. And I think that the arrests of large numbers of people without warrant or preventive detention is contrary to our own best system of government.

In a similar vein Professor Irving L. Horowitz, a sociologist and erstwhile panegyricist of Castro's Cuba until it began aiding the Palestinian terrorists against Israel, warned of overreacting to the problem of terrorism in the May, 1977, issue of *The Civil Liberties Review*, "Dangers to Liberty in Fighting Terrorism." According to Horowitz, "acceptance of some terrorism, like some protest violence, is a sign of a society's acceptance of the costs of liberty." Repeating the words of Walter Laqueur in *Guerrilla*, he maintains that "the hardware of the state is almost always greater, more pervasive, and more devastating than the disruptive possibilities that are available to terrorists."

In the light of our discussion in this work, that is manifestly untrue. For Horowitz, echoing now the words of J. Bowyer Bell, "there is scarcely any comparison between what terrorists achieve and the disruption caused by a major automobile accident on an urban superhighway. It is the traffic accident, Horowitz authoritatively tells us, that causes the far greater disruption. The real danger from terrorism lies in passing laws to combat it. "One has," Horowitz's voice seems to plead,

> a perfect right, even a duty, to raise questions about these new social costs of travel [frisking and baggage searches], certainly to inquire whether the new frisking procedures are permanent or transitory. Risk is a part of the nature of the democratic system — to permit modes of behavior that are uncontrolled and experimental. . . . Under the banner of the

anti-terrorist industry (airport-surveillance equipment, home-security systems, counter-terror research) enormous erosion of civil liberties could be made to seem all too rational and enlightened to the general public.

Horowitz's comments express the position of the professional civil libertarians. Their effect is to obscure from the American people the grave danger that threatens their most important right — life itself, without which all other rights are meaningless.

For example, some sources have disclosed that in 1965 a then much more radical Peoples Republic of China offered two nuclear bombs to Al Fatah. The donation was narrowly averted by CIA intervention. But now a thoroughly emasculated CIA would probably be unable to engage in such "dirty tricks," as a result of the efforts of our radicalized intelligentsia and their political puppets. After all, such an action by the CIA would be "illegal"; and if we need a CIA at all, we are told, it is only for intelligence-gathering, not clandestine operations.

As unstable a head of state as Qaddafi of Libya has also repeatedly vowed to obtain nuclear weapons. He certainly does not lack the wealth to obtain large numbers of the most sophisticated nuclear, chemical, and biological weapons. Since Libya under Qaddafi has also become a kind of international terrorist connection, the prospects are indeed foreboding.

Nonetheless, at the opening of the 1977 OAS Conference Secretary of State Cyrus Vance lectured the Latin American States against the use of "dirty tricks," and the like. He sermonized to the assembled delegates that their nations should respect human rights even when combating leftist terrorism (but not rightist terrorism?). Otherwise, governments will lose their moral authority. On the contrary, if governments show themselves unable to protect the very first right — to life — out of excessive sensitivity to lesser rights, they will lose all moral authority.

As the Chilean Foreign Minister correctly replied: "The real cause of supposed repression of human rights is not poverty or economic hardship, but subversion and terrorism sponsored by the Soviet Union. The problems of human rights and terrorism must be dealt with as one."

Despite Vance's public attitude, in the spring of 1977 the State Department released a statement saying that there is "every indication that international terrorism is on the increase." It identified Libya, Iraq, South Yemen, and Somalia as major centers of it. It also emphasized that the U.S. must develop a set of interagency guidelines for dealing with threats of nuclear, bacteriological, or chemical mass destruction. Assistant Secretary of State Bennett said that "we will have to prepare ourselves to deal with further attacks on American citizens and installations abroad, including those of American companies."

On the question of "dirty tricks," newly-appointed CIA Director Stansfield Turner was interviewed in *U.S. News & World Report* (May 16, 1977):

Q. Are covert operations — dirty tricks of that sort — really necessary?

A. We can't abandon covert action. However, in today's atmosphere, there is less likelihood that we would want to use this capability for covert action. But I can envisage circumstances in which the country might demand some covert action.

Q. What circumstances?

A. For instance, let's say a terrorist group appears with a nuclear weapon and threatens one of our cities and says, "If you don't give us some money or release some prisoners or do something, we will blow up Washington, D.C."

I think the country would be incensed if we did not have a covert-action capability to try to counter that — to go in and get the weapon or defuse it.

So, although we don't exercise it today, I think we must retain some capability for covert actions that range from small paramilitary operations to other actions that will influence events.

But by June, 1977, Carter Administration officials were testifying to Congress that the number of inquiries by the FBI into domestic security cases, including terrorist activities, had dropped under new bureau guidelines, to 214 from 4,868. The officials said they were eager to obtain guidelines from Congress on whether the bureau should continue such preventive investigations or limit itself to actual crimes. Deputy Assistant Attorney General Mary C. Lawton said, "The choice must be made and it must be made now." Representative Don Edwards (D. Calif.), Chairman of the House Civil Rights Subcommittee, sympathetically replied that he planned to move quickly on a bill that would limit the FBI to the investigation of actual crimes. He said it would include criminal conspiracy to commit bombings or terrorist acts, but would abolish the FBI's seperate domestic intelligence bureau.

In the face of this new megadeath technology, we now seem to be helpless. Lowell Ponte has argued that we are on the verge of another massive change in political and social structures similar to the ending of feudalism. Quite correctly he points to the major effect that technological developments in weaponry had on the feudal system. When the barbarians of that time went marauding through the area, everyone withdrew into the confines of the feudal castle, the center of the manorial system. The feudal oath was a contract. The serf promised obedience and a portion of his labor; the lord in turn promised him safety. But with gunpowder technology, just about any gang of dropouts or marginal people could drag a cannon up to the stone walls and blast a hole in them. The political systems that developed a gunpowder technology survived; the others became imperial appendages or disappeared. Thus, in the Middle East the gunpowder-using Ottoman Empire flourished, conquering all others with the exception of a Persian dynasty, which was also a gunpowder-using system. The incredible advances in modern technology seem to have produced an analogous condition today. But political and social structures have not as yet caught up with the conditions brought into being by technology. As presently constituted, they cannot, as the saying goes, cope with the problems — with the power now within the grasp of any gang of dropouts.

But many analysts betray a fundamental ignorance of Western republican political philosophy and political systems in offering solutions. Ponte, for example, warns that because of the threat or actuality of mass-death terrorism we will be tempted to relinquish our civil liberties in return for security provided by military and police power, that we will be willing to do *whatever* is necessary to detect and thwart would-be terrorists. We will accede to widespread telephone taps, mail openings, surveillance, punishment of dissent, preemptive arrest, and "perhaps even torture." To preclude the advent of such a "police system," we must, he urges, rethink the very structure of society. We must decentralize — decentralize everything — since terrorism thrives on centralization. We must all move away from the cities and lessen our dependence on technology everywhere. Despite the enormous cost involved, we must restructure into small, self-contained, self-sufficient units that produce everything necessary for life and culture, just as Buckminster Fuller has planned the future.

Well, at least Ponte has properly recognized the problem, which is more than most of our intellectuals who write of "the futility of terrorism" have done. I rather doubt, however, that the moral suasion of Mr. Ponte will be a force sufficient to constrain the elites to spend trillions to produce a Bucky Fuller-type society throughout the world. Even if accepted, it would take decades to realize. On the basis of the depressing chronicle presented here in regard to the threats of nuclear, chemical, biological, and other forms of technological terrorism, it is clear that what characterizes all elites is the lack of response. It is our firm prediction that nothing significant will be done — barring a wholesale circulation of elites — until it happens, probably several times. At that point in chaos everyone will be willing to accede to the very ugliest of totalitarian governments if it will only stop the horrors and once again restore order out of chaos.

A moderate alternative well worth our consideration is the ancient republican institution of crisis government. There are not, unfortunately, many alternatives available. In fact, crisis government seems to be the only one.

2. Ultimate Constitutional Remedies

THE best short introduction to crisis government, state of siege, or constitutional dictatorship may be found in *Constitutional Government and Democracy* (1968, first published in 1937) by Professor Carl J. Friedrich of Harvard. At the conclusion of a chapter on the subject in that work Friedrich explained that war and insurrection create the conditions of emergency that call for the establishment of constitutional dictatorship. He argues, in opposition to the view represented by Secretary Vance, that such powers should be in the hands of a military government:

> persons who would understand the nature of the world-revolutionary situation and would appreciate the limits of force in dealing with a conflict of this type. Constitutional dictatorship, on the surface a contradiction in terms, is the final test of constitutionalism. For a government which cannot meet emergencies is bound to fall sooner or later. There is no object in arguing against such emergency powers on the ground that they endanger the constitutional morale, and

hence the maintenance of the constitutional order. Of course they do. Any suspension of legal norms, no matter how temporary, raises doubts concerning their validity. But after all, what does an emergency mean if not that the constitutional order is threatened? Imminent invasion and civil war are only the most blatant and final stages of such a danger. No one in his right mind can argue that their emergence should not be forestalled. Unfortunately, no man can foretell the future. Hence, it will always be a matter of judgment, a matter of weighing risks as to which is more dangerous: the threatening emergency or the powers for combating it. Humanly enough, the more uncertain the choice, the more emphatic become the partisans. Nothing shows that more clearly than America's dilemma in the face of the world revolutionary situation. It is similar to the dilemma confronted in the rise of Hitler. Few would question in retrospect that even rather far-reaching measures designed to forestall that rise would have been in America's interest; yet at the time, in 1936, 1937, 1938, few were prepared to adopt such measures because they miscalculated the dangers ahead. Although modern industrialism forbids the employment of the Roman pattern of constitutional dictatorship, its underlying conceptions are still valid. Emergency powers should be very broad in scope, but the conditions for their exercise should be rigidly defined. The constitutional dictator should be appointed by a body which he does not in fact control, he should not be in a position to declare the emergency himself, and a fixed time limit should be attached to the grant of powers.

In 1948 Clinton Rossiter's *Constitutional Dictatorship: Crisis Government in the Moderr`Democracies* was published, the only full-length study of the institution in the English language. In a brief preface to the 1962 edition, Rossiter, by then one of the most prominent and influential of American political scientists, stated that he wished he had used the title "Crisis Government" rather than "Constitutional Dictatorship," the term "dictatorship" evidently having upset a number of his colleagues. He stated the theme of the work as follows:

> Instead of setting democracy against dictatorship, it proposes to demonstrate how the institutions and methods of dictatorship, have been used by the free men of the modern democracies during periods of severe national emergencies. It is written in frank recognition of a dangerous but inescapable truth: "No form of government can survive that excludes dictatorship when the life of the nation is at stake."

In the body of the work he deals with the Roman version, the Weimar Constitution, the French State of Siege, the British version (especially the Defense of the Realm Act), the American experience (especially under Lincoln and Roosevelt), and an overall evaluation of the institution. He describes the British Defense of the Realm Act as "the most radical parliamentary enactment in the history of England, indeed in all the history of constitutional government." He also maintains that the men who ruled England in 1940 "possessed arbitrary power such as the Tudors themselves did not enjoy, and the men who rule it in 1948 are equally able to claim such power should the nation again come to the crisis of war." Of the United States he wrote that "what Lincoln did, not what the Supreme Court said, is the precedent of the Constitution in the matter of presidential emergency power. Lincoln's actions form history's most illustrious precedent for constitutional dictatorship."

Rossiter's judgment on the value of the institution of constitutional dictatorship is clear in his parting words:

> If the crisis history of the modern democracies teaches us anything, it teaches us that power can be responsible, that strong government can be democratic government, that dictatorship can be constitutional. From this day forward we must cease wasting our energies in discussing whether the

government of the United States is to be powerful or not. It is going to be powerful or we are going to be obliterated. Our problem is to make that power effective and responsible, to make any future dictatorship a constitutional one. No sacrifice is too great for our democracy, least of all the temporary sacrifice of democracy itself.

More recently yet another American political scientist and a leading expert on the Presidency, Robert S. Hirschfield, chairman of the department at Hunter College and author of *The Power of the Presidency*, wrote a brief article on the subject, "Lessons of Lincoln's 'Dictatorship,' " in the *Times* (February 13, 1971). It is worth quoting at length:

Two basic principles of American crisis government were established during the Civil War. First, it was then made clear that to meet the challenge of a major emergency the barriers against omnipotent government established by the constitution must often be transcended. Preservation of the American system of constitutional rule is the ultimate purpose of a crisis regime, but it acknowledges no restrictions in assuming the authority needed to achieve that goal. In short, the power of a crisis government has no definable limits because its operational standard is necessity rather than constitutionality, to whatever extent the crisis demands, governmental authority will be expanded and concentrated and individual liberty will be circumscribed in time of emergency. The second principle is that the Presidency must always be the dominant organ of crisis government. Only the president can satisfy the crisis demand for unity, action, and leadership, for he is "the sole representative of all the people," and the only agency capable of responding quickly and decisively. . . . Later crisis presidents have invariably taken their cues from Lincoln's conception of emergency government. Thus, Wilson, Roosevelt, Truman, and Kennedy, though less averse [than Lincoln] to seeking congressional support for their policies, were always prepared to use extraconstitutional authority if they considered it necessary to effective defense of the nation. . . . Lincoln knew that a president who assumes the right to exercise plenary power is not a constitutional executive, and thus his only claim to legitimacy rests on the fact that his use of extraconstitutional authority is necessary to preserve the nation. Even more, he recognized that neither Congress nor the Supreme Court could effectively restrain the exercise of presidential emergency power, a fact which has been demonstrated on many occasions since the Civil War. . . . In so doing Lincoln focused attention on the most important lesson which contemporary Americans, living in an age characterized by crises, can learn: that crisis periods breed internal as well as external dangers to the preservation of a free society, and that while the immediate responsibility for meeting those dangers may rest with the nation's leaders, ultimately the people themselves must be prepared to defend their own freedom.

Logically there are but three possible positions on the subject of crisis government. One can argue that the democratic constitution contains within itself everything that is necessary to preserve the democratic state in a time of crisis, no matter how severe that crisis may be. That was the argument made by Justice Davis in the Milligan case, and reiterated by Senator Ervin at the time of the Watergate hearings, who termed it "the greatest decision that the Supreme Court of the United States has ever handed down." Rossiter emphatically disagreed with that position, noting that the decision was handed down after the end of the Civil War and two years after Lincoln's death. It was thus a rather hypocritical decision. Professor Corwin, another leading expert on the Presidency, also disagreed: "To suppose that such fustian would be of greater influence in determining presidential procedure in a future great emergency than precedents backed by the monumental reputation of Lincoln would be merely childish."

The second position is that crisis government is necessary for democratic systems, but that it is best left unconstitutional. The argument here is that by constraining the Chief Executive to act unconstitutionally you minimize the chances that he will be tempted to use the powers when it is not necessary to do so. The great statement for that position was given by John Locke toward the close of his *Second Treatise on Civil Government* (paragraphs 158-168):

> *Salus populi suprema lex* is certainly so just and fundamental a rule, that he who sincerely follows it cannot dangerously err. Where the legislative and executive power are in distinct hands, as they are in all moderated monarchies and well-framed governments, there the good of the society requires that several things should be left to the discretion of him that has the executive power . . . nay, many things there are which the law can by no means provide for, and that those must necessarily be left to the discretion of him that has the executive power in his hands, to be ordered by him as the public good and vantage shall require; nay, 'tis fit that the laws themselves should in some cases give way to executive power, or rather to this fundamental law of Nature and government — viz., that as much as may be, all the members of society are to be preserved. . . . This power to act according to discretion for the public good, without the prescription of the law and sometimes even against it, is that which is called prerogative. . . . For prerogative is nothing but the power of doing public good without a rule. The old question will be asked in this matter of prerogative. But who shall be the judge when this power is made right use of? . . . To this I reply, the people shall be the judge.

And that, whether by accident or design, is the current constitutional situation in the United States. But that condition too is fraught with danger. As Rossiter observed of Lincoln:

There is, however, this disturbing fact to remember: he set a precedent for bad men as well as good. It is just because Lincoln's reputation is so tremendous that a tyrant bent on illegal power might successfully appeal to this eminent shade for historical sanction of his own arbitrary actions. If Lincoln could calmly assert: "I conceived that I may, in any emergency, do things on a military ground which cannot constitutionally be done by congress," then some future president less democratic and less patriotic might assert the same thing.

And conversely, it assumes that the Chief Executive will be of sufficient intellectual and moral stature to be willing to violate the written constitution to preserve the nation, or, variantly, that he is not a subscriber to the first position.

Ironically, as the United States Senate debated emergency powers in the United States, the *Times* editorialized (August 28, 1974): "No one disputes the need for lodging emergency powers in the Chief Executive, a fact of political administration recognized as long ago as the seventeenth century in the writings of John Locke." It appears that the editors had never read John Locke's justification of the Chief Executive acting unconstitutionally.

The third possible position is that crisis government is necessary, but that it would be best, from the standpoint of ultimately preserving democratic liberties, if it were made constitutional. That was the position of the Romans. And the Romans, as Rossiter indicates, as far as we know, never violated the constitutional provisions in regard to the establishment of the dictatorship. With the notable exception of the United States, most democratic nations appear to have adopted the Roman position. Thus we find, in one form or another, various constitutional provisions for crisis government in Israel, Canada, the Republic of South Africa, Sweden, Switzerland, and most other democratic nations.

A U.S. Senate Special Committee on the Termination of
the National Emergency, co-chaired by Senators Church
of McC. Mathias, in November, 1973, issued its report,
"Emergency Powers Statutes: Provisions of Federal Law
Now in Effect Delegating to the Executive Extraordinary
Authority in Time of National Emergency." The introduction to the more than 600-page report began by casually
noting that a majority of the people of the United States
have lived all of their lives under emergency rule. As a
philosophical issue, it continued, the problem of how a
constitutional democracy reacts to great crises goes back
to the Greek city-states and the Roman Republic. Tracing
the American political theory of crisis government back to
John Locke, it concluded:

> The 2,000 year-old problem of how a legislative body in a
> democratic republic may extend extraordinary power for use
> by the executive during times of great crisis and dire
> emergency — but do so in ways assuring both that such
> necessary powers will be terminated immediately when the
> emergency has ended and that normal processes will be re-
> sumed — has not yet been resolved in this country. Too few
> are aware of the existence of emergency powers and their
> extent, and the problem has never been squarely faced.

Unfortunately, despite evidence to the contrary, the
senators succumbed to Kissinger-inspired fantasies about
détente:

> It is fortunate at this time that, when the fears and tensions
> of the cold war are giving way to relative peace and détente is
> now national policy, Congress can assess the nature, quality,
> and effect of what has become known as emergency powers
> legislation.

Congress too succumbed, and in September, 1976, President Ford signed the National Emergencies Act. In addition to ending the emergencies then in effect, the act

greatly limited the powers the President could invoke in any future emergency. This occurred at the very time when the world was experiencing an escalation of terrorism and some experts were warning of a coming widespread use of technological weapons of mass destruction by terrorists.

The problem facing the United States today — and the West in general — is survival. The question is whether we can survive without some form of crisis government as we try to deal with mass, doomsday terrorism.

Since the Enlightenment modern revolutions have been characterized by the efforts to extend them to other nations, to extend them in time, and especially by the totalitarian scope of the revolution — the effort to revamp all aspects of life entirely, to effect a radical transvaluation of values in politics, ethics, religion, art, literature, culture, social and familial organization, economics, and all other areas. Despite that historical record, as well as the leading analyses of revolution, the glorificatory myth continues that revolutions are the ultimate expression of democracy: mass spontaneous upheavals, not elite-manipulated, which occur when the patience of the common man is exhausted, and which issue in greater freedom, democracy, and economic well-being, and that they overthrow tyrannical regimes by heroically defeating the despot's armed forces as the democratic mob courses through the streets. All of these beliefs are demonstrably false. Yet the myth remains ascendant.

Virtually all contemporary revolutions and movements, especially since World War II, have had as their ultimate goal the destruction of Western civilization and the United States in particular, which is seen as the head of the monster of imperialism whose tentacles encircle the globe. In the face of that mortal threat to its existence, the West has been crippled by a corrosive and corrupt ideology-morality that causes our political-intellectual elites to declare themselves in sympathy with, and in support of, the very elements that boldly proclaim their goal to be the destruction of the West. A brilliant literary portrayal of that attitude was presented by Jean Raspail in his *The Camp of the Saints*, a novel that has been systematically suppressed in the United States. Those elites are characterized by the lack of a moral-political will to use the power at their command. As C.L. Sulzberger gloomily observed in the *Times* (December 15, 1976), after describing the prevalence of that détente-inspired attitude in the West, the most sophisticated weapons systems in the world are of no use unless there exists the willingness to use them. The course of our destruction has thus been paved by a radicalized academic-media-political complex, and its ultimate result will be the destruction of civilization as we know it. The solution at this date, it appears, can only be a crisis government in some form, under the guidance of a completely new elite characterized by a dedication to preserve Western civilization and not bound by absurd chivalric scruples in their efforts to do so.

In the light of what terrorists are willing to do and what their goal is (the destruction of the United States and Western civilization), it does not seem possible to survive without using some form of crisis government.

The alternative course is an endless one of permanent revolution. And that is because its intention is to create "the new socialist man," and its means is the "healthy" injection of terror into the system by the revolutionary government until human nature is totally revamped. But if human nature is unchanging, as the leading Western political philosophers and theologians maintain, then it is revolution without end.

The paralysis of will caused by legalistic and moral scruples, as well as by liberal masochism, is nowhere better exemplified than by Idi Amin. Presented with a black tyrant who massacred hundreds of thousands of blacks, who slit his enemies' throats and drank their blood and ate their vital organs, the Western world could do no more than wring its hands, pass resolutions, and not talk too much about the atrocities in the media. Space instead given to attacks on Chile, Rhodesia, and South Africa.

Our antistatist intellectuals and journalists, left and right, have deprived us of the will to mount an adequate *political* defense of our political system at this time. Winston Churchill more than hinted at such a conclusion in his reflective history of the Second World War and of the early postwar period: "I have called this volume *Triumph and Tragedy*," he explained, "because the overwhelming victory of the grand alliance has failed so far to bring general peace to our anxious world." Mindful of the follies of appeasement in the thirties, he had begun the book by defining the "Theme of the Volume" under a subheading that read: "How The Great Democracies Triumphed, And So Were Able To Resume The Follies Which Had So Nearly Cost Them Their Life."

In a speech in New York City Aleksandr I. Solzhenitsyn expressed similar sentiments:

> Is it possible or impossible to compare the experience of those who have suffered to those who have not suffered? Is it ever possible to warn anyone of oncoming danger? How many witnesses have come to your country, how many waves of immigration, all warning you of the same experiences and the same dangers? Yet these proud skyscrapers still stand, and you go on believing that it will not happen here. Only when it happens to you will you know it is true.

Without a change of personnel in our ruling elites, as well as a radical revamping of the prevailing political values, we are evidently doomed to await passively its happening here. Then, finally, as Solzhenitsyn says, we'll know it is true. Out of fear of authoritarian discipline sustained by a genuinely nationalist crisis government, we will have purchased totalitarian slavery.

SELECT BIBLIOGRAPHY

Journals and Periodicals

Assets Protection. The Territorial Imperative, Inc., Madison, Wis.

Beres, Louis René. *"Hic Sunt Dracones*: The Nuclear Threat of International Terrorism," *Parameters* (Journal of the U.S. Army War College), vol. IX, no. 2, June, 1979, pp. 11-19.
——— "The Threat of Nuclear Terrorism in the Middle East," *Current History*, vol. 70, no. 412.

Centre d'Information et de Documentation de la L.I.L.B.P., 24 Wavre, Belgium.
Cherico, P. "Security Requirements and Standards for Nuclear Power Plants," *Security Management*, vol. 18, no. 6: 22-24.

Drake, Elisabeth, and Reid, Robert C. "The Importation of Liquefied Natural Gas," *Scientific American*, April 1977.

Flood, Michael. "Nuclear Sabotage," *Bulletin of the Atomic Scientists*, September 1976.
FBI Law Enforcement Bulletin.

Idso, Sherwood B. "Israel Possesses Up to 60,000 Tons of Uranium," *Los Angeles Times*, October 9, 1975.
Ingram, Timothy H. "Peril of the Month: Gas Supertankers," *Washington Monthly*, February 1973.
Institute for the Study of Conflict, London. Publishes *Conflict Studies* six times a year, each issue dealing with a specific movement or area. Also publishes *Special Reports* on critical movements or situations, and an annual, *Power and Conflict*, an overall assessment of the world strategic situation, with substantial emphasis on terrorism.

Intersearch. A twice-monthly newsletter published by International Terrorist Research Center, El Paso, Texas. It is intended primarily for business corporations.

Jenkins, Brian. "Research Note: Rand's Research on Terrorism," *Terrorism, An International Journal,* vol. I, no. 1, 1977, pp. 85-95.

Lapp, Ralph E. "The Ultimate Blackmail," *The New York Times Magazine,* February 4, 1973, pp. 13, 29-34.

Macdonald, Gordon J.F. "How to Wreck the Environment," in *Unless Peace Comes,* ed. Nigel Calder. N.Y.: Viking, 1968.

McGuire, E. Patrick. "International Terrorism and Business Security," *The Conference Board Information Bulletin,* No. 65, Oct. 1979, 22 pp.

Mengel, R.W. "The Impact of Nuclear Terrorism on the Military's Role in Society," in *International Terrorism,* ed. M. Livingston, q.v.

National Criminal Justice Reference Service, Washington, D.C.
National Technical Information Service, Springfield, Va.

Police Chief, International Association of Chiefs of Police, Gaithersburg, Md.
Police Journal, Sussex, England.

Rand Corporation, Santa Monica, Calif.
RISK International, Inc., Alexandria, Va. Publishes a monthly eight-page summary on patterns and trends in terrorism. Also publishes a regional risk assessment six times a year. Subscribers to its service can request information on particular problems. It describes itself as the nation's first privately computerized data base on terrorist activities, with the capacity to extrapolate information on any terrorist organization or activities in any major city or country. Operated by two former high-level Air Force intelligence officers, its data base is reputedly the best inside or outside the government.

Roberts, Kenneth E. "Terrorism and the Military Response," Strategic Studies Institute, U.S. Army War College, October 14, 1975.

Security Gazette, London.
Security Management, American Society for Industrial Security, Washington, D.C.
Singer, Michael, Weir, David, and Canfield, Barbara Newman. "Nuclear Nightmare: America's Worst Fears Come True," *New York*, Nov. 26, 1979, pp. 43-49.
Sundberg, Jacob. "The Antiterrorist Legislation in Sweden," in *International Terrorism*, ed. M. Livingston, q.v.

Terrorism, An International Journal. Crane, Russak & Co., N.Y., since 1977. Contributors include government officials in the area and academic specialists.
Top Security, Twentieth Century Security Education, Surrey, England.

Waters, Mike. "FPC Bares Loss of Gas Tank Data," *Washington Post*, July 13, 1973.
Watkins, Frederick M. "The Problem of Constitutional Dictatorship," *Public Policy I* (Annual Yearbook of Harvard University Graduate School of Public Administration), 1939, pp. 324-379.
Willrich, Mason. "Terrorists Keep Out!" *Bulletin of the Atomic Scientists*, May 1975.

Government Documents

Congressional Reference Service Seminar Report on LNG Hazards, January 1979.
Emergency Powers Statutes: Provisions of Federal Law Now in Effect Delegating to the Executive Extraordinary Authority in Time of National Emergency. Report of the Special Committee on the Termination of the National Emergency, U.S. Senate, Nov. 1973. 607 pp.
Investigation of Charges Relating to Nuclear Reactor Safety. Vol. I, Hearings and Appendixes, 1,076 pp., Joint Committee on Atomic Energy, 94th Cong., 2nd sess., 1976. Discusses the allegation that there has been a suppression of safety information within the NRC.

218/ TECHNOLOGICAL TERRORISM

LEAA Report of March 2, 1977. National Advisory Committee on Criminal Justice Standards and Goals. 661 pp. See esp. the section on technological terrorism by R.W. Mengel.
Liquefied Energy Gases Safety. 3 vols. GAO, July 1978.
On the Transportation of Liquefied Natural Gas. Office of Technology Assessment, September 1977.
Protecting Special Nuclear Material in Transit: Improvements Made and Existing Problems. GAO, 1974.
Report on Strategic Special Nuclear Material Inventory Differences. ERDA, 1977. 229 pp.
Summary of Executive Orders in Times of War and National Emergency: A Working Paper. Special Committee on National Emergencies and Delegated Emergency Powers, U.S. Senate, Aug. 1974. 69 pp.
Terrorism, Selected Bibliography. 2nd ed. LEAA, U.S. Dept. of Justice, March 1977. Contains 168 annotated entries and how to obtain them.

Books and Monographs

Barron, John. *KGB: The Secret Work of Soviet Secret Agents*. New York: Bantam, 1974.

Crozier, Brian. *A Theory of Conflict*. New York: Scribner's, 1974.

Evans, Ernest. *Calling A Truce to Terror: The American Response to International Terrorism*. Westport, Conn.: Greenwood Press, 1979.

Friedlander, Robert A. *Terrorism: Documents of International and Local Control* (2 vols.). New York: Oceana Press, 1978.

Hirschfield, Robert S. *The Power of the Presidency*. Chicago: Aldine, 1973.

Jenkins, Brian M. *The Consequences of Nuclear Terrorism*. Santa Monica, Cal.: Rand Corporation, Aug. 1979.

——— *High-Technology Terrorism and Surrogate Warfare*. Rand, Jan. 1975.
——— *The Potential for Nuclear Terrorism*. Rand, May 1977.
——— *Will Terrorists Go Nuclear?* Rand, Nov. 1975.

International Terrorism in the Contemporary World, ed. by Marius H. Livingston. Westport, Conn.: Greenwood Press, 1978.

Kupperman, Robert, and Trent, Darrell. *Terrorism: Threat, Reality Response*. Stanford, Cal.: Hoover Institution Press, 1979.

Lear, John. *Recombinant DNA, The Untold Story*. New York: Crown, 1978.
Linde, Peter van der, with Hintze, Naomi A. *Time Bomb, LNG: the Truth about Our Newest and Most Dangerous Energy Source*. New York: Doubleday, 1978.

McPhee, John. *The Curve of Binding Energy*. New York: Ballantine, 1975.
Miller, Arthur S. *Presidential Power*. St. Paul, Minn.: West Publishing Co., 1977.

Parker, Donn B. *Crime by Computer*. New York: Scribner's, 1976.
Possony, Stefan T., and Bouchey, L. Francis. *International Terrorism — The Communist Connection — with a Case Study of West German Terrorist Ulrike Meinhof*. American Council for World Freedom, 1978.

Rogers, Lindsay. *Crisis Government*. New York: W.W. Norton, 1934.
Rosenthal, A.M., and Gelb, A. *The Night the Lights Went Out*. New York: New American Library, 1965.
Rossiter, Clinton L. *Constitutional Dictatorship: Crisis Government in Modern Democracies*. New York: Harcourt, Brace, and World, 1962.

Stevenson, William. *A Man Called Intrepid*. New York: Ballantine, 1976.

Trinquier, Roger (Col.). *Modern Warfare: A French View of Counterinsurgency*. New York: Praeger, 1964.

Watkins, Frederick M. *The Failure of Constitutional Emergency Powers under the German Republic*. Cambridge, Mass.: Harvard University Press, 1939.
Whiteside, Thomas. *Computer Capers*. New York: Crowell, 1978.
Willrich, Mason, and Taylor, Theodore B. *Nuclear Theft: Risks and Safeguards*. Cambridge, Mass.: Ballantine, 1974.

About the Author

Richard Charles Clark, who received his doctorate from Columbia University, is Associate Professor of Government and Politics at St. John's University on Long Island, New York, where his courses on Revolution, Current Terrorism, and Crisis Government have attracted wide attention. His extracurricular activities include serving as Book Editor of the *Review of National Literatures* and Senior Editor of the newsletter "State of the Nation," published by the Bagehot Research Council.